BE
RIGHT

BE
RIGHT

HOW TO BE RIGHT WITH GOD, YOURSELF, AND OTHERS

NT COMMENTARY

ROMANS

Warren W. Wiersbe

David C Cook®

transforming lives together

BE RIGHT
Published by David C. Cook
4050 Lee Vance View
Colorado Springs, CO 80918 U.S.A.

David C. Cook Distribution Canada
55 Woodslee Avenue, Paris, Ontario, Canada N3L 3E5

David C. Cook U.K., Kingsway Communications
Eastbourne, East Sussex BN23 6NT, England

David C. Cook and the graphic circle C logo
are registered trademarks of Cook Communications Ministries.

Unless otherwise noted, all Scripture quotations are taken from the King James Version of the
Bible. (Public Domain.) Scripture quotations marked NASB are taken from the *New American
Standard Bible*, © Copyright 1960, 1995 by The Lockman Foundation. Used by permission; NIV
are taken from the *Holy Bible, New International Version*®. *NIV*®. Copyright © 1973, 1978, 1984
International Bible Society. Used by permission of Zondervan. All rights reserved; WMS are taken
from *The New Testament in the Language of the People* by Charles B. Williams, © 1966 by Edith S.
Williams. Used by permission of Moody Press, Moody Bible Institute of Chicago; and ESV are
taken from *The Holy Bible, English Standard Version*. Copyright © 2000; 2001 by Crossway
Bibles, a division of Good News Publishers. Used by permission. All rights reserved.

LCCN 2008924756
ISBN 978-1-4347-6847-6
eISBN 978-1-4347-6585-7

© 1977 Warren W. Wiersbe

First edition of *Be Right* by Warren W. Wiersbe published by Victor Books®
in 1977 © Warren W. Wiersbe, ISBN 0-89693-778-X

The Team: Gudmund Lee, Amy Kiechlin, Jack Campbell, and Susan Vannaman
Series Cover Design: John Hamilton Design
Cover Photo: Getty Stockbyte

Printed in the United States of America
Second Edition 2008

7 8 9 10 11 12 13 14

060111

Dedicated to
David
Carolyn
Bob
and Judy
with their father's
love and appreciation

CONTENTS

THE BIG IDEA

An Introduction to *Be Right*
by Ken Baugh

Even if you aren't a die-hard UCLA basketball fan, you have to admire coach John Wooden. He is a living legend in college basketball, having coached the UCLA Bruins from 1948–1975, during which time he won ten NCAA national championships. He has won more titles than any coach in the history of the game. One of my prized possessions is a basketball signed by Coach Wooden; it sits in a glass case on a shelf in my office. I might have to sell the ball some day to pay for my girl's college education, but right now I keep it as a reminder of what made him so great. You might be asking, "Why is he so special?" The answer is simple: He was relentless in coaching his players on the fundamentals of the game.

I had the privilege to attend one of Coach Wooden's basketball camps at Point Loma College in San Diego during my sophomore year in high school. I remember one morning, I woke up early and looked out my dorm-room window to see Coach Wooden walking around the outdoor courts with the tallest man I had ever seen in my life. Later that morning, I asked one of the coaches I was working with what Coach Wooden was doing, and he told me that professional basketball players from all over would come to seek Coach Wooden's advice if they were in a slump. That advice always consisted of only one thing: fundamentals.

You see, Coach Wooden would not tolerate flashy basketball. Rather, his practices would consist of drill after drill designed to help his players master the fundamentals—things like defense, dribbling, how to make good passes, and the proper form for a jump shot. It's even been said that on the first day of practice before every new season, Coach Wooden would instruct his players on the proper way to put on their socks and tie their shoes so they wouldn't get blisters. He left nothing to chance. Reinforcing the fundamentals of basketball was the secret to Coach Wooden's great success.

Periodically, I believe that every follower of Christ needs to get back to the basics of their Christian faith as well—and what better way to do that than by studying the book of Romans? Martin Luther said that Romans is "the chief part of the New Testament." John Calvin wrote, "When anyone gains a knowledge of this epistle he has an entrance opened to him to all the most hidden treasures of Scripture." And John Chrysostom, considered by many to be the greatest preacher of the third century, said, "Romans is unquestionably the fullest, deepest compendium of all sacred foundational truths." Clearly the book of Romans is essential to anyone wishing to better understand the foundations of the Christian faith, as it addresses things like sanctification, justification, the deity of Jesus Christ, and the forgiveness of sin. And yet, in the midst of all of that important and life-changing information, there exists a central theme—one "BIG IDEA" to tie it all together: the righteousness of God.

When we say that God is righteous, what we mean is that He is the standard by which we measure all other things. In his *Systematic Theology*, Dr. Wayne Grudem puts it this way: "God's righteousness means that God always acts in accordance with what is right and is Himself the final standard of what is right" (Zondervan, 1995; 203). This is an important concept to grasp because in this day and age many people have convinced themselves that there are no absolute standards, believing that people can do whatever they want to do as long as nobody gets hurt. But God's Word makes it clear that there *is* a measure by which everything else will be judged, and that measure is perfection. Paul says,

> There is no one righteous, not even one; there is no one who understands, no one who seeks God. All have turned away, they have together become worthless; there is no one who does good, not even one ... for all have sinned and fall short of the glory of God. (Rom. 3:10–12, 23 NIV)

Therefore, if God is righteous and His standard is perfection, yet we are imperfect, then we have a big problem. Unfortunately, that problem is called sin, and if we're not careful it will result in separating us from God for all eternity. Thankfully, though, we also have a God who is gracious and seeks to redeem us through a relationship with His Son, Jesus Christ. In 2 Corinthians 5:21 Paul tells us, "God made him who had no sin to be sin for us, so that in him we might become the righteousness of God." In this way, Paul says, our spirits can be renewed and we can find "eternal life in Christ Jesus our Lord" (Rom. 6:23).

So the book of Romans not only reinforces the fundamentals of the Christian faith, but it also declares the nature of God as both righteous and gracious. Should you read this commentary and study the book of Romans? Yes, a thousand times yes! But more than just study it, you should come back to it again and again so that your faith may remain founded on sound doctrine. It is in this way that will build your house of faith on a solid foundation (Luke 6:48), and avoid becoming like children who are "tossed to and fro by the waves and carried about by every wind of doctrine" (Eph. 4:14 ESV).

***

Dr. Wiersbe's commentaries have been a source of guidance and strength to me over the many years that I have been a pastor. His unique style is not overly academic, but theologically sound. He explains the deep truths of Scripture in a way that everyone can understand and apply. Whether you're a Bible scholar or a brand-new believer in Christ, you will benefit, as I have, from Warren's insights. With your Bible in one hand and Dr. Wiersbe's commentary in the other, you will be able to accurately unpack the deep truths of God's Word and learn how to apply them to your life.

Drink deeply, my friend, of the truths of God's Word, for in them you will find Jesus Christ, and there is freedom, peace, assurance, and joy.

—Ken Baugh
Pastor of Coast Hills Community Church
Aliso Viejo, California

A Word from the Author

If you are tired of all the wrong things in your life, in the lives of others, and in this world, then Paul's epistle to the Romans is the book for you.

The theme of Romans is the righteousness of God. In this letter, Paul tells how to *Be Right*—with God, ourselves, and others. Paul also explains how one day God will make creation right and bring peace on earth.

The epistle to the Romans was not written for woolgatherers or religious sightseers. You will have to *think* as you study this letter, but the rewards will be worth the efforts. If you understand Romans, you will have the key to understanding the rest of the Bible. Better still, you will have the secret to successful Christian living.

Be Right is not a detailed explanation of Romans. It is an expository survey that helps you understand the main message of the letter and how it applies to your life today. After you have mastered this book, you can turn to the more detailed commentaries and, I trust, be better prepared to benefit from them.

—Warren W. Wiersbe

A Suggested Outline of the Book of Romans

Theme: The righteousness of God

Key verse: Romans 1:17

I. Introduction (Romans 1:1–17)

II. Sin—Righteousness Demanded (Romans 1:18—3:20)

    A. The Gentile world is guilty (Romans 1:18–32)

    B. The Jewish world is guilty (Romans 2:1—3:8)

    C. The whole world is guilty (Romans 3:9–20)

III. Salvation—Righteousness Declared (Romans 3:21—5:21)

    A. Justification explained (Romans 3:21–31)

    B. Justification illustrated in Abraham (Romans 4)

    C. Justification explained in Adam (Romans 5)

IV. Sanctification—Righteousness Defended (Romans 6—8)

    A. Victory—the flesh (Romans 6)

    B. Liberty—the Law (Romans 7)

    C. Security—the Spirit (Romans 8)

V. Sovereignty—Righteousness Declined (Romans 9—11)

    A. Israel's past riches (Romans 9)

    B. Israel's present rejection (Romans 10)

    C. Israel's future restoration (Romans 11)

VI. Service—Righteousness Demonstrated (Romans 12:1—15:7)

    A. In the church body (Romans 12)

    B. In society (Romans 13)

    C. Toward the weaker believer (Romans 14:1—15:7)

VII. Conclusion (Romans 15:8—16:27)

Chapter One

READY FOR ROME

(Romans 1:1–17)

O
n May 24, 1738, a discouraged missionary went "very unwillingly" to a religious meeting in London. There a miracle took place. "About a quarter before nine," he wrote in his journal, "I felt my heart strangely warmed. I felt I did trust in Christ, Christ alone, for salvation; and an assurance was given me that He had taken away my sins, even mine, and saved me from the law of sin and death."

That missionary was John Wesley. The message he heard that evening was the preface to Martin Luther's commentary on Romans. Just a few months before, John Wesley had written in his journal: "I went to America to convert the Indians; but Oh! who shall convert me?" That evening in Aldersgate Street, his question was answered. And the result was the great Wesleyan Revival that swept England and transformed the nation.

Paul's epistle to the Romans is still transforming people's lives, just the way it transformed Martin Luther and John Wesley. The one Scripture above all others that brought Luther out of mere religion into the joy of salvation by grace, through faith, was Romans 1:17: "The just shall live by faith." The Protestant Reformation and the Wesleyan Revival were both the fruit of this wonderful letter written by Paul from

Corinth about the year AD 56. The letter was carried to the Christians at Rome by one of the deaconesses of the church at Cenchrea, Sister Phebe (Rom. 16:1).

Imagine! You and I can read and study the same inspired letter that brought life and power to Luther and Wesley! And the same Holy Spirit who taught them can teach us! You and I can experience revival in our hearts, homes, and churches if the message of this letter grips us as it has gripped people of faith in centuries past.

In the opening verses of the letter, Paul introduces himself to the believers in Rome. Some of them must have known him personally, since he greets them in the final chapter, but many of them he had never met. So in these first seventeen verses, Paul seeks to link himself to his Roman readers in three ways.

1. HE PRESENTED HIS CREDENTIALS (1:1–7)

In ancient days, the writer of a letter always opened with his name. But there would be many men named Paul in that day, so the writer had to further identify himself and convince the readers that he had a right to send the letter. What were Paul's credentials?

He was a servant of Jesus Christ (v. 1a). The word Paul used for *servant* would be meaningful to the Romans, because it is the word *slave*. There were an estimated sixty million slaves in the Roman Empire, and a slave was looked on as a piece of property, not a person. In loving devotion, Paul had enslaved himself to Christ, to be His servant and obey His will.

He was an apostle (v. 1b). This word means "one who is sent by authority with a commission." It was applied in that day to the representatives of the emperor or the emissaries of a king. One of the requirements for an apostle was the experience of seeing the risen Christ (1 Cor. 9:1–2). Paul saw Christ when he was on the road to Damascus (Acts 9:1–9), and it was then that Christ called him to be His apostle to the Gentiles. Paul received from Christ divine revelations that he was to share with the churches.

He was a preacher of the gospel (vv. 1c–4). When he was a Jewish rabbi, Paul was separated as a Pharisee to the laws and traditions of the Jews. But when he yielded to Christ, he was separated to the gospel and its ministry. *Gospel* means "the good news." It is the message that Christ died for our sins, was buried and rose again, and now is able to save all who trust Him (1 Cor. 15:1–4). It is "the gospel of God" (Rom. 1:1) because it originates with God; it was not invented by humans. It is "the gospel of Christ" (Rom. 1:16) because it centers in Christ, the Savior. Paul also calls it "the gospel of his Son" (Rom. 1:9), which indicates that *Jesus Christ is God.* In Romans 16:25–26, Paul called it "my gospel." By this he meant the special emphasis he gave in his ministry to the doctrine of the church and the place of the Gentiles in the plan of God.

The gospel is not a new message; it was promised in the Old Testament, beginning in Genesis 3:15. The prophet Isaiah certainly preached the gospel in passages such as Isaiah 1:18 and chapters 53 and 55. The salvation we enjoy today was promised by the prophets, though they did not fully understand all that they were preaching and writing (1 Peter 1:10–12).

Jesus Christ is the center of the gospel message. Paul identified Him as a man, a Jew, and the Son of God. He was born of a virgin (Isa. 7:14; Matt. 1:18–25) into the family of David, which gave Him the right to David's throne. He died for the sins of the world and then was raised from the dead. It is this miraculous event of substitutionary death and victorious resurrection that constitutes the gospel, and it was this gospel that Paul preached.

He was a missionary to the Gentiles (vv. 5–7). *Missionary* is the Latin form of "apostle—one who is sent." There were probably several assemblies of believers in Rome and not just one church, since in Romans 16 Paul greets a number of "home church" groups (Rom. 16:5, 10–11, 14). We do not know for certain how these churches began, but it is likely that believers from Rome who were at Pentecost established the assemblies on their return to Rome (Acts 2:10). There were both Jews and Gentiles in these fellowships, because Paul addresses both in this letter. (Jews: Rom. 2:17–29; 4:1; 7:1. Gentiles: Rom. 1:13; 11:13–24; 15:15–21.) The churches in Rome were not founded by Peter or any other apostle. If they had been, Paul would not have planned to visit Rome, because his policy was to minister only where no other apostle had gone (Rom. 15:20–21).

Note the repetition of the word *called:* Paul was called to be an apostle; the believers were the called of Jesus Christ; and they were also called saints. (Not "to be" saints; they already were saints! A saint is a set-apart one, and the person who trusts Jesus Christ is set apart and is a saint.) Salvation is not something that we do for God; it is God who calls us in His grace (2 Thess. 2:13–14). When you trust Christ, you are saved by His grace and you experience His peace.

Paul's special commission was to take the gospel to the Gentiles (the word *nations* means Gentiles), and this is why he was planning to go to Rome, the very capital of the empire. He was a preacher of the gospel, and the gospel was for all nations. In fact, Paul was anxious to go to Spain with the message of Christ (Rom. 15:28).

Having presented his credentials, Paul proceeded to forge a second link between himself and the believers in Rome.

2. HE EXPRESSED HIS CONCERN (1:8–15)

We can well understand Paul's concern for the churches that *he* founded, but why would he be concerned about the believers at Rome? He was unknown to many of them, yet he wanted to assure them that he was deeply concerned about their welfare. Note the evidences of Paul's concern.

He was thankful for them (v. 8). "The whole world"—meaning the whole Roman Empire—knew of the faith of the Christians at Rome. Travel was relatively common in that day and "all roads led to Rome." It is no wonder that the testimony of the church spread abroad, and this growing witness made Paul's ministry easier as he went from place to place and was able to point to this testimony going out from the heart of the Roman Empire.

He prayed for them (vv. 9–10). They did not know of Paul's prayer support, but the Lord knew about it and honored it. (I wonder how many of us know the people who are praying for us?) One of the burdens of Paul's prayer was that God would permit him to visit Rome and minister to the churches there. He would have visited them sooner, but his missionary work had kept him busy (Rom. 15:15–33). He was about to leave Corinth for Jerusalem to deliver the special offering received from the Gentile churches for the poor Jewish saints. He hoped he would be able to travel from Jerusalem to Rome, and then on to Spain, and he was hoping for a prosperous journey.

Actually, Paul had a very perilous journey, and he arrived in Rome a prisoner as well as a preacher. In Jerusalem he was arrested in the temple, falsely accused by the Jewish authorities, and eventually sent to Rome as the emperor's prisoner to be tried before Caesar. When Paul wrote this letter, he had no idea that he would go through imprisonment and even shipwreck before arriving in Rome. At the close of the letter (Rom. 15:30–33), he asked the believers in Rome to pray for him as he contemplated this trip, and it is a good thing that they did pray.

He loved them (vv. 11–12). "I long to see you." This is the pastor's heart in Paul the great missionary. Some of the saints in Rome were very dear to Paul, such as Priscilla and Aquila (Rom. 16:3–4), who risked their lives for him, "the beloved Persis" (Rom. 16:12), and others who had labored and suffered with Paul. But he also loved the believers that he did not know, and he longed to be able to share some spiritual gift with them. He was looking forward to a time of mutual blessing in the love of Christ.

He was in debt to them (vv. 13–14). As the apostle to the Gentiles, Paul had an obligation to minister in Rome. He would have fulfilled that obligation sooner, but his other labors had hindered him. Sometimes Paul was hindered because of the work of Satan (1 Thess. 2:17–20), but in this case he was hindered because of the work of the Lord. There was so much to do in Asia Minor and Greece that he could not immediately spare time for Rome. But Paul had to pay his debt; he was under orders from the Lord.

The Greeks considered every non-Greek a barbarian. Steeped in centuries of philosophy, the Greeks saw themselves as wise and everyone else as foolish. But Paul felt an obligation to *all* men, just as we need to feel a burden for the whole world. Paul could not be free from his debt until he had told as many people as possible the good news of salvation in Christ.

He was eager to visit them (v. 15). Two different Greek words are translated "ready" in the King James Version. One means "prepared," as in Acts 21:13. "I am ready ... to die at Jerusalem for the name of the Lord Jesus." The other one, used in Romans 1:15, means "eager, with a ready mind." Paul was not eager to die, though he was prepared to die. But he was eager to visit Rome that he might minister to the believers there. It was not the eagerness of a sightseer, but the eagerness of a soul winner.

After reading these five evidences of Paul's concern for the Christians at Rome, these saints could not but give thanks to God for the apostle Paul and his burden to come and minister to them. Actually, the epistle to the Romans, in which Paul explained the gospel he preached, was his letter of introduction that prepared the believers for his visit. No doubt the false teachers had already gotten to Rome and were seeking to poison the Christians against Paul. Some would accuse him of being antilaw; others would say he was a traitor to the Jewish nation. Still others would twist his teaching about grace and try to prove that he taught loose living (see Rom. 3:8). No wonder Paul was eager to get to Rome! He wanted to share with them the fullness of the gospel of Christ.

But would the gospel of Christ work in the great city of Rome as it had in other places? Would Paul succeed there, or would he fail? The apostle no doubt felt these objections and raised these questions in his own mind, which is why he forged a third link between himself and his readers.

3. HE AFFIRMED HIS CONFIDENCE (1:16–17)

What a testimony: "I am a debtor! I am eager! I am not ashamed!" Why would Paul even be tempted to be ashamed of the gospel as he contemplated his trip to Rome? For one thing, the gospel was identified with a poor Jewish carpenter who was crucified. The Romans had no special appreciation for the Jews, and crucifixion was the lowest form of execution given a criminal. Why put your faith in a Jew who was crucified?

Rome was a proud city, and the gospel came from Jerusalem, the capital city of one of the little nations that Rome had conquered. The Christians in that day were not among the elite of society; they were common people and even slaves. Rome had known many great philosophers and philosophies; why pay any attention to a fable about a Jew who arose from the dead (1 Cor. 1:18–25)? Christians looked on each other as brothers and sisters, all one in Christ, which went against the grain of Roman pride and dignity. To think of a little Jewish tentmaker going to Rome to preach such a message is almost humorous.

But Paul was not ashamed of the gospel. He had confidence in his message, and he gave us several reasons that explain why he was not ashamed.

The origin of the gospel: It is the gospel of Christ (v. 16a). Any message that was handed down from Caesar would immediately get the attention of the Romans. But the message of the gospel is from and about the very Son of God! In his opening sentence, Paul called this message "the gospel of God" (Rom. 1:1). How could Paul be ashamed of such a message, when it came from God and centered in His Son, Jesus Christ?

During my years in high school, I was chosen to be an office monitor. The other hall monitors sat at various stations around the building, but I was privileged to sit right outside the door of the main high school office. I was entrusted with important messages that I had to deliver to different teachers and staff members, and on occasion even to other schools. Believe me, it was fun to walk into a classroom and even interrupt a lesson. No teacher ever scolded me, because all of them knew I carried messages from the principal. I never had to be afraid or ashamed, because I knew where my messages came from.

The operation of the gospel: It is the power of God (v. 16b). Why be ashamed of power? Power is the one thing that Rome boasted of the most. Greece might have its philosophy, but Rome had its power. The fear of Rome hovered over the empire like a cloud. Were they not the conquerors? Were not the Roman legions stationed all over the known world? But with all of her military power, Rome was still a weak nation. The philosopher Seneca called the city of Rome "a cesspool of iniquity"; and the writer Juvenal called it a "filthy sewer into which the dregs of the empire flood."

No wonder Paul was not ashamed: He was taking to sinful Rome the one message that had the power to change people's lives! He had seen the gospel work in other wicked cities, such as Corinth and Ephesus, and he was confident that it would work in Rome. It had transformed his own life, and he knew it could transform the lives of others. There was a third reason why Paul was not ashamed.

The outcome of the gospel: It is the power of God unto salvation (v. 16c). That word *salvation* carried tremendous meaning in Paul's day. Its basic meaning is "deliverance," and it was applied to personal and national deliverance. The emperor was looked on as a savior, as was the physician who healed you of illness. The gospel delivers sinners from the penalty and power of sin. Salvation is a major theme in this letter; salvation is the great need of the human race (see Rom. 10:1, 9–10). If men and women are to be saved, it must be through faith in Jesus Christ as proclaimed in the gospel.

The outreach of the gospel: "to everyone that believeth" (vv. 16d–17). This was not an exclusive message for either the Jew or the Gentile; it was for all people, *because everyone needs to be saved.* "Go ye into all the world, and preach the Gospel," was Christ's commission (Mark 16:15). "To the Jew first" does not suggest that the Jew is better than the Gentile, for there is "no difference" in condemnation or in salvation (Rom. 2:6–11; 10:9–13). The gospel came "to the Jew first" in the ministry of Jesus Christ (Matt. 10:5–7) and the apostles (Acts 3:24–26). How marvelous it is to have a message of power that can be taken to *all* people!

God does not ask people to *behave* in order to be saved, but to *believe.* It is faith in Christ that saves the sinner. Eternal life in Christ is one gift that is suitable for all people, no matter what their need may be or what their station in life.

Romans 1:17 is the key verse of the letter. In it Paul announces the theme: "the righteousness of God." The word *righteousness* is used in one way or another over sixty times in this letter (*righteous, just,* and *justified*). God's righteousness is revealed in the gospel; for in the death of Christ, God revealed His righteousness by punishing sin; and in the resurrection of

Christ, He revealed His righteousness by making salvation available to the believing sinner. The problem "How can a holy God ever forgive sinners and still be holy?" is answered in the gospel. Through the death and resurrection of Christ, God is seen to be both "just, and the justifier" (Rom. 3:26).

The gospel reveals a righteousness that is *by faith*. In the Old Testament, righteousness was *by works*, but sinners soon discovered they could not obey God's law and meet His righteous demands. Here Paul refers to Habakkuk 2:4: "The just shall live by his faith." This verse is quoted three times in the New Testament: Romans 1:17; Galatians 3:11; and Hebrews 10:38. Romans explains "the just"; Galatians explains "shall live"; and Hebrews explains "by faith." There are more than sixty references to faith or unbelief in Romans, because the only way a sinner can become just before God is "by faith."

When you study Romans, you walk into a courtroom. First, Paul called Jews and Gentiles to the stand and found both guilty before God. Then he explained God's marvelous way of salvation—justification by faith. At this point, he answered his accusers and defended God's salvation. "This plan of salvation will encourage people to sin!" they cry. "It is against the very law of God!" But Paul refuted them, and in so doing explained how the Christian can experience victory, liberty, and security.

Chapters 9—11 are not a parenthesis or a detour. There were Jewish believers in the Roman assemblies, and they would naturally ask, "What about Israel? How does God's righteousness relate to the Jews in this new age of the church?" In these three chapters, Paul gave a complete history of Israel—past, present, and future.

Then he concluded with the practical outworking of God's righteousness in the life of the believer. This begins with dedication to God (Rom. 12:1–2), continues with ministry in the church (Rom. 12:3–21), and then obedience to the government (Rom. 13:1–14). He also told Jews and Gentiles, strong and weak, how to live together in harmony and joy. In the closing section (Rom. 15:14—16:27), Paul explained his plans and greeted his friends.

When you sum it all up, the book of Romans is saying to us, *"Be right!"* Be right with God, with yourself, and with others. The righteousness of God received by faith makes it possible for us to live right lives. Rome needed this message, and we need it today: *Be right!*

QUESTIONS FOR PERSONAL REFLECTION
OR GROUP DISCUSSION

1. What was the background of the people and the church at Rome?

2. Where did the letter to the Romans come from?

3. What is the main theme and purpose of this book?

4. How is the title *Be Right* related to the verse "The just shall live by faith"?

5. What were Paul's credentials? If you were writing a letter to a church, how would you introduce yourself?

6. What are some evidences in Romans 1:8–15 that Paul was concerned for the believers?

7. What evidences do you display that you are concerned for others?

8. What were some obstacles to faith for Romans living at that time? How did Paul encourage them?

9. How did Paul show that he was not ashamed of the gospel? What do you think about this?

10. In what way is the gospel "the power of God"? How does this affect how you live out your faith in your daily life?

Chapter Two

WHEN GOD GIVES UP

(Romans 1:18—3:20)

Hear ye! Hear ye! Court is now in session!" Paul could have used those awesome words at this point in his letter, because Romans 1:18 is the door that leads us into God's courtroom. The theme of Romans is the righteousness of God, but Paul had to begin with the unrighteousness of humankind. Until a person knows he is a sinner, he cannot appreciate the gracious salvation God offers in Jesus Christ. Paul followed the basic Bible pattern: first law and condemnation, then grace and salvation.

In this section, God makes three declarations that together prove that all people are sinners and need Jesus Christ.

1. THE GENTILE WORLD IS GUILTY! (1:18–32)

The picture Paul paints here is an ugly one. I confess that there are some neighborhoods that I dislike driving through, and I avoid them if I can. My avoiding them does not change them or eliminate them. God's description of sinners is not a pretty one, but we cannot avoid it. This section does not teach evolution (that humans started low and climbed high), but *devolution:* He started high and, because of sin, sank lower than the beasts. Four stages mark humankind's tragic devolution.

(1) Intelligence (vv. 18–20). Human history began with people knowing God. Human history is not the story of a beast that worshipped idols, and then evolved into a person worshipping one God. Human history is just the opposite: People began knowing God but turned from the truth and rejected God. God revealed Himself to humankind through creation, the things that He made. From the world around them, humans knew that there was a God who had the wisdom to plan and the power to create. Humans realized too that this Creator was eternal … "His eternal power and Godhead" (Rom. 1:20), since God could not be created if He is the Creator. These facts about God are not hidden in creation; they are "clearly seen" (v. 20). "The heavens declare the glory of God; and the firmament sheweth his handiwork" (Ps. 19:1).

The word translated "hold" in Rom. 1:18 can also be translated "hold down, suppress." Men knew the truth about God, but they did not allow this truth to work in their lives. They suppressed it in order that they might live their own lives and not be convicted by God's truth. The result, of course, was refusing the truth (Rom. 1:21–22), and then turning the truth into a lie (Rom. 1:25). Finally, humankind so abandoned the truth that they became like beasts in their thinking and in their living.

(2) Ignorance (vv. 21–23). Humans knew God; this is clear. But they did not *want* to know God or honor Him as God. Instead of being thankful for all that God had given them, humans refused to thank God or give Him the glory He deserves. They were willing to use God's gifts, but they were not willing to worship and praise God for His gifts. The result was an empty mind and a darkened heart. Man the worshipper became man the philosopher, but his empty wisdom only revealed his foolishness. Paul summarized all of Greek history in one dramatic statement: "the times of this ignorance" (Acts 17:30). First Corinthians 1:18–31 is worth reading at this point.

Having held down God's truth and refusing to acknowledge God's glory, humankind was left without a god, and humankind is so constituted that they must worship something. If they will not worship the true God, they will worship a false god, *even if they have to manufacture it themselves.* This fact about humankind accounts for their propensity to idolatry. They exchanged the glory of the true God for substitute gods that they themselves made. They exchanged glory for shame, incorruption for corruption, truth for lies.

Note that first on the list of false gods is *ourselves.* This fulfilled Satan's purpose when he told Eve, "You will be like God" (Gen. 3:5 NASB). "Glory to man in the highest!" Satan encouraged humans to say. Instead of man being made in God's image, man made gods in his own image—and then descended so low as to worship birds, beasts, and bugs.

(3) Indulgence (vv. 24–27). From idolatry to immorality is just one short step. If man is his own god, then he can do whatever he pleases and fulfill his desires without fear of judgment. We reach the climax of man's battle with God's truth when man exchanges the truth of God for "the lie" and abandons truth completely. "The lie" is that man is his own god, and he should worship and serve himself and not the Creator. It was "the lie" Satan used in the garden to lead Eve into sin: "Ye shall be as gods." Satan has always wanted the worship that belongs only to God (Isa. 14:12–15; Matt. 4:8–10), and in idolatry, he receives that worship (1 Cor. 10:19–21).

The result of this self-deification was self-indulgence, and here Paul mentions a vile sin that was rampant in that day and has become increasingly prevalent in our own day: homosexuality. This sin is repeatedly condemned in Scripture (Gen. 18:20ff.; 1 Cor. 6:9–10; Jude 7). Paul characterizes it as "vile" and "unnatural," as well as "against nature." Not only were the men guilty, but "even the women."

Because of their sin "God gave them up" (Rom. 1:24, 26), which means that He permitted them to go on in their sins and reap the sad consequences.

They received "in their own persons the due penalty of their error" (Rom. 1:27 NASB). This is the meaning of Romans 1:18: "The wrath of God is being revealed from heaven" (literal translation). God revealed His wrath, not by sending fire from heaven, but by abandoning sinful men to their lustful ways. But there was one more stage.

(4) Impenitence (vv. 28–32). When man began to feel the tragic consequences of his sins, you would think he would repent and seek God, but just the opposite was true. Because he was abandoned by God, he could only become worse. Man did not even want to retain God in his knowledge! So, "God gave them over" this time to a "depraved mind" (Rom. 1:28 NASB), which means a mind that cannot form right judgments. They now abandoned themselves to sin. Paul names twenty-four specific sins, all of which are with us today. (For other lists, see Mark 7:20–23; Gal. 5:19–21; 1 Tim. 1:9–10; 2 Tim. 3:2–5.)

But the worst is yet to come. Men not only committed these sins in open defiance of God, but encouraged others and applauded them when they sinned. How far man fell! He began glorifying God but ended exchanging that glory for idols. He began knowing God but ended refusing to keep the knowledge of God in his mind and heart. He began as the highest of God's creatures, made in the image of God, but he ended lower than the beasts and insects, because he worshipped them as his gods. The verdict? "They are without excuse" (Rom. 1:20).

This portion of Scripture gives ample proof that the heathen are lost. Dan Crawford, British missionary to Africa, said: "The heathen are sinning against a flood of light." There is a desperate need for us to carry the gospel to all men, for this is the only way they can be saved.

2. THE JEWISH WORLD IS GUILTY! (2:1—3:8)

Bible scholars do not agree on whom Paul was addressing in Romans

2:1–16. Some think he was dealing with the moral pagan who did not commit the sins named in Romans 1:18–32, but who sought to live a moral life. But it seems to me that Paul was addressing his Jewish readers in this section. To begin with, his discussion of the law in Romans 2:12–16 would have been more meaningful to a Jew than to a Gentile. And in Romans 2:17, he openly addressed his reader as "a Jew." This would be a strange form of address if in the first half of the chapter he were addressing Gentiles.

It would not be an easy task to find the Jews guilty, since disobedience to God was one sin they did not want to confess. The Old Testament prophets were persecuted for indicting Israel for her sins, and Jesus was crucified for the same reason. Paul summoned four "witnesses" to prove the guilt of the Jewish nation.

(1) The Gentiles (2:1–3). Certainly the Jews would applaud Paul's condemnation of the Gentiles in Romans 1:18–32. In fact, Jewish national and religious pride encouraged them to despise the "Gentile dogs" and have nothing to do with them. Paul used this judgmental attitude to prove the guilt of the Jews, for the very things they condemned in the Gentiles, they themselves were practicing! They thought that they were free from judgment because they were God's chosen people. But Paul affirmed that God's election of the Jews made their responsibility and accountability even greater.

God's judgment is according to truth. He does not have one standard for the Jews and another for the Gentiles. One who reads the list of sins in Romans 1:29–32 cannot escape the fact that each person is guilty of at least one of them. There are "sins of the flesh and of the spirit" (2 Cor. 7:1); there are "prodigal sons" and "elder brothers" (Luke 15:11–32). When they condemned the Gentiles for their sins, the Jews were really condemning themselves. As the old saying puts it, "When you point your finger at somebody else, the other three are pointing at you."

(2) God's blessing (2:4–11). Instead of giving the Jews special treatment from God, the blessings they received from Him gave them greater responsibility to obey Him and glorify Him. In His goodness, God had given Israel great material and spiritual riches: a wonderful land, a righteous law, a temple and priesthood, God's providential care, and many more blessings. God had patiently endured Israel's many sins and rebellions, and had even sent them His Son to be their Messiah. Even after Israel crucified Christ, God gave the nation nearly forty more years of grace and withheld His judgment. It is not the judgment of God that leads men to repentance, but the goodness of God—but Israel did not repent.

In Romans 2:6–11, Paul was not teaching salvation by character or good deeds. He was explaining another basic principle of God's judgment: God judges according to deeds, just as He judges according to truth. Paul was dealing here with the consistent actions of a person's life, the total impact of his character and conduct. For example, David committed some terr   ins, but the total emphasis of his life was obedience to God. Judas confessed his sin and supplied the money for buying a cemetery for strangers, yet the total emphasis of his life was disobedience and unbelief.

True saving faith results in obedience and godly living, even though there may be occasional falls. When God measured the deeds of the Jews, He found them to be as wicked as those of the Gentiles. The fact that the Jews occasionally celebrated a feast or even regularly honored the Sabbath day did not change the fact that their consistent daily life was one of disobedience to God. God's blessings did not lead them to repentance.

(3) God's law (1:12–24). Paul's statement in Romans 2:11, "For there is no respect of persons with God," would shock the Jews, for they considered themselves deserving of special treatment because they were chosen by God. But Paul explained that the Jewish law only made the guilt of Israel that much greater. God did not give the law to the Gentiles, so they would not be judged by the law. Actually, the Gentiles had "the work of the law written in their hearts" (Rom. 2:15). Wherever you go, you find people with an inner sense of right and wrong, and this inner judge, the Bible calls "conscience." You find among all cultures a sense of sin, a fear of judgment, and an attempt to atone for sins and appease whatever gods are feared.

The Jew boasted in the law. He was different from his pagan neighbors who worshipped idols. But Paul made it clear that it was not the *possession* of the law that counted, but the *practice* of the law. The Jews looked on the Gentiles as blind, in the dark, foolish, immature, and ignorant. But if God found the "deprived" Gentiles guilty, how much more guilty were the "privileged" Jews. God not only judges according to truth (Rom. 2:2), and according to men's deeds (Rom. 2:6), but He also judges "the secrets of men" (Rom. 2:16). He sees what is in the heart.

The Jewish people had a religion of outward action, not inward attitude. They may have been moral on the outside, but what about the heart? Our Lord's indictment of the Pharisees in Matthew 23 illustrates the principle perfectly. God not only sees the deeds but He also sees the "thoughts and intents of the heart" (Heb. 4:12). It is possible for a Jew to be guilty of theft, adultery, and idolatry (Rom. 2:21–22) even if no one saw him commit these sins outwardly. In the Sermon on the Mount we are told that such sins can be committed in the heart.

Instead of glorifying God among the Gentiles, the Jews were dishonoring God, and Paul quoted Isaiah 52:5 to prove his point. The pagan Gentiles had daily contact with the Jews in business and other activities, and they were not fooled by the Jews' devotion to the law. The very law that the Jews claimed to obey only indicted them!

(4) Circumcision (2:25–29). This was the great mark of the covenant, and it had its beginning with Abraham, the father of the Jewish nation (Gen. 17). To the Jews, the Gentiles were "uncircumcised dogs." The tragedy is that the Jews depended on this physical mark instead of the spiritual reality it represented (Deut. 10:16; Jer. 9:26; Ezek. 44:9). A true Jew is one who has had an inward spiritual experience in the heart, and not merely an outward physical operation. People today make this same mistake with reference to baptism or the Lord's Supper, or even church membership.

God judges according to "the secrets of men" (Rom. 2:16), so that He is not impressed with mere outward formalities. An obedient Gentile with no circumcision would be more acceptable than a disobedient Jew with circumcision. In fact, a disobedient Jew turns his circumcision into uncircumcision in God's sight, for God looks at the heart. The Jews praised each other for their obedience to the law, but the important thing is the "praise of God" and not the praise of men (Rom. 2:29). When you recall that the name "Jew" comes from "Judah," which means "praise," this statement takes on new meaning (Gen. 29:35; 49:8).

Paul's summation (3:1–8). All of Paul's four witnesses agreed: The Jews were guilty before God. In Romans 3:1–8, Paul summed up the argument and refuted those Jews who tried to debate with him. They raised three questions: (1) "What advantage is it to be a Jew?" Reply: Every advantage, especially possessing the Word of God; (2) "Will Jewish unbelief cancel God's faithfulness?" Reply: Absolutely not—it establishes it; (3) "If our sin commends His righteousness, how can He judge us?" Reply: We do not do evil that good may come of it. God judges the world righteously.

3. The Whole World Is Guilty! (3:9–20)

The third declaration was obvious, for Paul had already proved (charged) both Jews and Gentiles to be guilty before God. Next he declared that all people were sinners, and proved it with several quotations from the Old Testament. Note the repetition of the words *none* and *all*, which in themselves assert the universality of human guilt.

His first quotation was from Psalm 14:1–3. This psalm begins with "The fool hath said in his heart, 'There is no God.'" The words "there is" are in italics, meaning they were added by the translators; so you can read the sentence, "The fool hath said in his heart, 'No, God!'" This parallels the description of man's devolution given in Romans 1:18–32, for it all started with man saying no to God.

These verses indicate that the whole of man's inner being is controlled by sin: his mind ("none that understandeth"), his heart ("none that seeketh after God"), and his will ("none that doeth good"). Measured by God's perfect righteousness, no human being is sinless. No sinner seeks after God. Therefore, God must seek the sinner (Gen. 3:8–10; Luke 19:10). Man has gone astray and has become unprofitable both to himself and to God. Our Lord's parables in Luke 15 illustrate this perfectly.

In Romans 3:13–18, Paul gave us an X-ray study of the lost sinner, from head to foot. His quotations are as follows: verse 13a—Psalm 5:9; verse 13b—Psalm 140:3; verse 14—Psalm 10:7; verses 15–17—Isaiah 59:7–8; verse 18—Psalm 36:1. These verses need to be read in their contexts for the full impact.

Romans 3:13–14 emphasize human speech—the throat, tongue, lips, and mouth. The connection between words and character is seen in Matthew 12:34: "For out of the abundance of the heart the mouth speaketh." The sinner is spiritually dead by nature (Eph. 2:1–3), therefore only death can come out of his mouth. The condemned mouth can become a converted mouth and acknowledge that "Jesus is Lord" (Rom. 10:9–10 NIV). "For by thy words thou shalt be justified, and by thy words thou shalt be condemned" (Matt. 12:37).

In Romans 3:15–16, Paul pictured the sinner's feet. Just as his words are deceitful, so his ways are destructive. The Christians' feet are shod with the gospel of peace (Eph. 6:15), but the lost sinner brings death, destruction, and misery wherever he goes. These tragedies may not occur immediately, but they will come inevitably. The lost sinner is on the broad road that leads to destruction (Matt. 7:13–14); he needs to repent, trust Jesus Christ, and get on the narrow road that leads to life.

Romans 3:17 deals with the sinner's mind: He does not know the way of God's peace. This is what caused Jesus to weep over Jerusalem (Luke 19:41–44). The sinner does not want to know God's truth (Rom. 1:21, 25, 28); he prefers to believe Satan's lie. God's way of peace is through Jesus Christ: "Therefore being justified by faith, we have peace with God through our Lord Jesus Christ" (Rom. 5:1).

In Romans 3:18, which cites Psalm 36:1, the sinner's arrogant pride is prescribed: "There is no fear of God before their eyes." The entire psalm should be read to get the full picture. The ignorance mentioned in Romans 3:17 is caused by the pride of verse 18, for it is "the fear of the LORD" that is the beginning of knowledge (Prov. 1:7).

These quotations from God's law, the Old Testament Scriptures, lead to one conclusion: The whole world is guilty before God. There may be those who want to argue, but every mouth is stopped. There is no debate or defense. The whole world is guilty, Jews and Gentiles. The Jews stand condemned by the law of which they boast, and the Gentiles stand condemned on the basis of creation and conscience.

The word *therefore* in Romans 3:20 carries the meaning of "because," and gives the reason why the whole world is guilty. No flesh can obey God's law and be justified (declared righteous) in His sight. It is true that "the doers of the law shall be justified" (Rom. 2:13), but nobody can do what the law demands. This inability is one way that people know they are sinners. When they try to obey the law, they fail miserably and need to cry out for God's mercy. Neither Jew nor Gentile can obey God's law; therefore God must save sinners by some other means. The explanation of that means by which people can be saved occupied Paul for the rest of his letter.

The best way to close this section would be to ask a simple question: Has your mouth ever been stopped? Are you boasting of your own self-righteousness and defending yourself before God? If so, then perhaps you have never been saved by God's grace. It is only when we stand silent before Him as sinners that He can save us. As long as we defend ourselves and commend ourselves, we cannot be saved by God's grace. The whole world is guilty before God—and that includes you and me.

QUESTIONS FOR PERSONAL REFLECTION
OR GROUP DISCUSSION

1. How do you feel when you see or hear the words "you are guilty"? Why?

2. Why do people not want to admit their guilt? How have you experienced this in your own life?

3. What four stages of "devolution" are described? What was the cause?

4. Why do people suppress the truth about God? When have you struggled with this?

5. Why is this just one short step from idolatry to immorality?

6. What does it mean that, because of people's sin, God "gave them up" or God "gave them over" (1:24, 28)?

7. Who or what are the witnesses that prove the guilt of the Jewish nation?

8. At the time of the writing of Romans, what displeased God the most about the Jews?

9. Instead of special treatment, what did God's blessings actually give the Jews? How might this be true for God's blessings to you?

10. What does Romans 3:10 ("There is none who does good," NASB) mean to you when you see people who seem to be good people doing good deeds? Why would Paul say something like this?

Chapter Three

FATHER ABRAHAM

(Romans 3:21—4:25)

[handwritten annotation: never changes]

[handwritten annotation: Justification – God declares sinner righteous in christ]

[handwritten annotation: Sanctification – God makes the believer more like Christ (may change day to day)]

Paul's theme in the second section of his letter was salvation—righteousness declared. He proved that all people are sinners; so his next goal was to explain how sinners can be saved. The theological term for this salvation is *justification by faith*. Justification is the act of God whereby He declares the believing sinner righteous in Christ on the basis of the finished work of Christ on the cross. Each part of this definition is important, so we must consider it carefully.

To begin with, justification is an act, not a process. There are no degrees of justification; each believer has the same right standing before God. Also, justification is something God does, not man. No sinner can justify himself before God. Most important, justification does not mean that God makes us righteous, but that He declares us righteous. Justification is a legal matter. God puts the righteousness of Christ on our record in the place of our own sinfulness. And nobody can change this record.

Do not confuse justification and sanctification. Sanctification is the process whereby God makes the believer more and more like Christ. Sanctification may change from day to day. Justification never changes. When the sinner trusts Christ, God declares him righteous, and that declaration will never be repealed. God looks on us and deals with us as though we had never sinned at all!

But how can the holy God declare sinners righteous? Is justification merely a fictional idea that has no real foundation? In this section of Romans, Paul answered these questions in two ways. First, he explained justification by faith (Rom. 3:21–31); then he illustrated justification by faith from the life of Abraham (Rom. 4:1–25).

1. JUSTIFICATION EXPLAINED (3:21–31)

"But now the righteousness of God ... has been manifested" (Rom. 3:21, literal translation). God revealed His righteousness in many ways before the full revelation of the gospel: His law, His judgments against sin, His appeals through the prophets, His blessing on the obedient. But in the gospel, a new kind of righteousness has been revealed (Rom. 1:16–17), and the characteristics of this righteousness are spelled out in this section.

Apart from the law (v. 21). Under the Old Testament law, righteousness came by people behaving, but under the gospel, righteousness comes by believing. The law itself reveals the righteousness of God, because the law is "holy, and just, and good" (Rom. 7:12). Furthermore, the law bore witness to this gospel righteousness even though it could not provide it. Beginning at Genesis 3:15, and continuing through the entire Old Testament, witness is given to salvation by faith in Christ. The Old Testament sacrifices, the prophecies, the types, and the great "gospel Scriptures" (such as Isa. 53) all bore witness to this truth. The law could witness to God's righteousness, but it could not provide it for sinful humanity. Only Jesus Christ could do that (see Gal. 2:21).

Through faith in Christ (v. 22a). Faith is only as good as its object. All people trust something, if only themselves, but the Christian trusts Christ. Law righteousness is a reward for works. Gospel righteousness is a gift through faith. Many people say, "I trust in God!" But this is not what saves us. It is personal, individual faith in Jesus Christ that saves and justifies the lost sinner. Even the demons from hell believe in God and tremble, yet this does not save them (James 2:19).

For all men (vv. 22b–23). God gave His law to the Jews, not to the Gentiles, but the good news of salvation through Christ is offered to all men. All men need to be saved. There is no difference between the Jew and the Gentile when it comes to condemnation. "All have sinned, and are coming short of the glory of God" (Rom. 3:23, literal translation). God declared everyone guilty so that He might offer everyone His free gift of salvation.

By grace (v. 24). God has two kinds of attributes: absolute (what He is in Himself), and relative (how He relates to the world and men). One of His absolute attributes is love: "God is love" (1 John 4:8). When God relates that love to you and me, it becomes grace and mercy. God in His mercy does not give us what we do deserve, and God in grace gives us what we do not deserve. The Greek word translated "freely" is translated in John 15:25 as "without a cause." We are justified without a cause! There is no cause in us that would merit the salvation of God! It is all of grace!

At great cost to God (vv. 24b–25). Salvation is free, but it is not cheap. Three words express the price God paid for our salvation: *propitiation*, *redemption*, and *blood*. In human terms, "propitiation" means appeasing someone who is angry, usually by a gift. But this is not what it means in the Bible. "Propitiation" means the satisfying of God's holy law, the meeting of its just demands, so that God can freely forgive those who come to Christ. The word *blood* tells us what the price was. Jesus had to die on the cross in order to satisfy the law and justify lost sinners.

The best illustration of this truth is the Jewish Day of Atonement described in Leviticus 16. Two goats were presented at the altar, and one of them was chosen for a sacrifice. The goat was slain and its blood taken into the Holy of Holies and sprinkled on the mercy seat, that golden cover on the ark of the covenant. This sprinkled blood covered the two tablets of the law inside the ark. The shed blood met (temporarily) the righteous demands of the holy God.

The priest then put his hands on the head of the other goat and confessed the sins of the people. Then the goat was taken out into the wilderness and set free to symbolize the carrying away of sins. "As far as the east is from the west, so far hath he removed our transgressions from us" (Ps. 103:12). In the Old Testament period, the blood of animals could never take away sin; it could only cover it until the time when Jesus would come and purchase a finished salvation. God had "passed over" the sins that were past (Rom. 3:25, literal translation), knowing that His Son would come and finish the work. Because of His death and resurrection, there would be "redemption"—a purchasing of the sinner and setting him free.

Dr. G. Campbell Morgan was trying to explain "free salvation" to a coal miner, but the man was unable to understand it. "I have to pay for it," he kept arguing.

With a flash of divine insight, Dr. Morgan asked, "How did you get down into the mine this morning?"

"Why, it was easy," the man replied. "I just got on the elevator and went down."

Then Morgan asked, "Wasn't that too easy? Didn't it cost you something?"

The man laughed. "No, it didn't cost me anything, but it must have cost the company plenty to install that elevator." Then the man saw the truth: "It doesn't cost me anything to be saved, but it cost God the life of His Son."

In perfect justice (vv. 25–26). God must be perfectly consistent with Himself. He cannot break His own law or violate His own nature. "God is love" (1 John 4:8), and "God is light" (1 John 1:5). A God of love wants to forgive sinners, but a God of holiness must punish sin and uphold His righteous law. How can God be both "just and the justifier"? The answer is in Jesus Christ. When Jesus suffered the wrath of God on the cross for the sins of the world, He fully met the demands of God's law and also fully expressed the love of God's heart. The animal sacrifices in the Old Testament never took away sin, but when Jesus died, He reached all the way back to Adam and took care of those sins. No one (including Satan) could accuse God of being unjust or unfair because of His seeming passing over of sins in the Old Testament time.

To establish the law (vv. 27–31). Because of his Jewish readers, Paul wanted to say more about the relationship of the gospel to the law. The doctrine of justification by faith is not against the law, because it establishes the law. God obeyed His own law in working out the plan of salvation. Jesus in His life and death completely fulfilled the demands of the law. God does not have two ways of salvation, one for the Jews and one for the Gentiles, for He is one God. He is consistent with His own nature and His own law. If salvation is through the law, then men can boast, but the principle of faith makes it impossible for men to boast. The swimmer, when he is saved from drowning, does not brag because he trusted the lifeguard. What else could he do? When a believing sinner is justified by faith, he cannot boast of his faith, but he can boast in a wonderful Savior.

In Romans 4—8, Paul explained how God's great plan of salvation was in complete harmony with the Old Testament Scriptures. He began first with the father of the Jewish nation, Abraham.

2. JUSTIFICATION ILLUSTRATED (4:1–25)

The Jewish Christians in Rome would immediately have asked, "How does this doctrine of justification by faith relate to our history? Paul, you say that this doctrine is witnessed to by the law and the prophets. Well, what about Abraham?"

Paul accepted the challenge and explained how Abraham was saved. Abraham was called "our father," referring primarily to the Jews' natural and physical descent from Abraham. But in Romans 4:11, Abraham was also called "the father of all them that believe," meaning all who have trusted Christ (see Gal. 3:1–18). Paul stated three important facts about Abraham's salvation that prove that the patriarch's spiritual experience was like that of believers today.

(1) He was justified by faith, not works (vv. 1–8). Paul called two witnesses to prove that statement: Moses (Gen. 15:6) and David (Ps. 32:1–2). In Romans 4:1–3, Paul examined the experience of Abraham as recorded in Genesis 15. Abraham had defeated the kings (Gen. 14) and was wondering if they would return to fight again. God appeared to him and assured him that He was his shield and "exceeding great reward" (Gen. 15:1). But the thing that Abraham wanted most was a son and heir. God had promised him a son, but as yet the promise had not been fulfilled.

It was then that God told him to look at the stars. "So shall thy seed [descendants] be!" God promised (v. 5), and Abraham believed God's promise. The Hebrew word translated *believed* means "to say amen." God gave a promise, and Abraham responded with "Amen!" It was this faith that was counted for righteousness.

The word *counted* in Romans 4:3 is a Greek word that means "to put to one's account." It is a banking term. This same word is used eleven times in this chapter, translated "reckoned" (Rom. 4:4, 9–10) and "imputed" (Rom. 4:6, 8, 11, 22–24), as well as "counted." When a man works, he earns a salary and this money is put to his account. But Abraham did not work for his salvation; he simply trusted God's Word. It was Jesus Christ who did the work on the cross, and His righteousness was put on Abraham's account.

Romans 4:5 makes a startling statement: God justifies the ungodly! The law said, "I will not justify the wicked" (Ex. 23:7). The Old Testament judge was commanded to "justify the righteous, and condemn the wicked" (Deut. 25:1). When Solomon dedicated the temple, he asked God to condemn the wicked and justify the righteous (1 Kings 8:32). But God justifies the ungodly—because there are no godly for Him to justify! He put our sins on Christ's account that He might put Christ's righteousness on our account.

In Romans 4:6–8, Paul used David as a witness, quoting from one of David's psalms of confession after his terrible sin with Bathsheba (Ps. 32:1–2). David made two amazing statements: (1) God forgives sins and imputes righteousness apart from works; (2) God does not impute *Count* our sins. In other words, once we are justified, our record contains Christ's perfect righteousness and can never again contain our sins. Christians do sin, and these sins need to be forgiven if we are to have fellowship with God (1 John 1:5–7), but these sins are not held against us. God does keep a record of our good works, so that He might reward us when Jesus comes, but He is not keeping a record of our sins.

(2) He was justified by grace, not law (vv. 9–17). As we have seen, the Jews gloried in circumcision and the law. If a Jew was to become righteous before God, he would have to be circumcised and obey the law. Paul had already made it clear in Romans 2:12–29 that there must be an inward obedience to the law, and a "circumcision of the heart." Mere external observances can never save the lost sinner.

But Abraham was declared righteous when he was in the state of uncircumcision. From the Jewish point of view, Abraham was a Gentile. Abraham was ninety-nine years old when he was circumcised (Gen. 17:23–27).

This was more than fourteen years after the events in Genesis 15. The conclusion is obvious: Circumcision had nothing to do with his justification.

Then why was circumcision given? It was a sign and a seal (Rom. 4:11). As a sign, it was evidence that he belonged to God and believed His promise. As a seal, it was a reminder to him that God had given the promise and would keep it. Believers today are sealed by the Holy Spirit of God (Eph. 1:13–14). They have also experienced a spiritual circumcision in the heart (Col. 2:10–12), not just a minor physical operation, but the putting off of the old nature through the death and resurrection of Christ. Circumcision did not add to Abraham's salvation; it merely attested to it.

But Abraham was also justified before the law was given, and this fact Paul discusses in Romans 4:13–17. The key word here is "promise." Abraham was justified by believing God's promise, not by obeying God's law, for God's law through Moses had not yet been given. The promise to Abraham was given purely through God's grace. Abraham did not earn it or merit it. So today, God justifies the ungodly because they believe His gracious promise, not because they obey His law. The law was not given to save people, but to show them that they need to be saved (Rom. 4:15).

The fact that Abraham was justified by grace and not law proves that salvation is for all. Abraham is the father of all believers, both Jews and Gentiles (Rom. 4:16; Gal. 3:7, 29). Instead of the Jew complaining because Abraham was not saved by law, he ought to rejoice that God's salvation is available to all men, and that Abraham has a spiritual family (all true believers) as well as a physical family (the nation of Israel). Paul saw this as a fulfillment of Genesis 17:5: "A father of many nations have I made thee."

(3) He was justified by resurrection power, not human effort (vv. 18–25). These verses are an expansion of one phrase in Romans 4:17: "who quickeneth the dead." Paul saw the rejuvenation of Abraham's body as a picture of resurrection from the dead, and then he related it to the resurrection of Christ.

One reason why God delayed in sending Abraham and Sarah a son was to permit all their natural strength to decline and then disappear. It was unthinkable that a man ninety-nine years old could beget a child in the womb of his wife who was eighty-nine years old! From a reproductive point of view, both of them were dead.

But Abraham did not walk by sight; he walked by faith. What God promises, He performs. All we need do is believe. Abraham's initial faith in God as recorded in Genesis 15 did not diminish in the years that followed. In Genesis 17—18, Abraham was "strong in faith." It was this faith that gave him strength to beget a son in his old age.

The application to salvation is clear: God must wait until the sinner is "dead" and unable to help himself before He can release His saving power. As long as the lost sinner thinks he is strong enough to do anything to please God, he cannot be saved by grace. It was when Abraham admitted that he was "dead" that God's power went to work in his body. It is when the lost sinner confesses that he is spiritually dead and unable to help himself that God can save him.

The gospel is "the power of God unto salvation" (Rom. 1:16) because of the resurrection of Jesus Christ from the dead. Romans 4:24 and Romans 10:9–10 parallel each other. Jesus Christ was "delivered up to die on account of our offenses, and was raised up because of our justification" (Rom. 4:25, literal translation). This means that the resurrection of Christ is the proof that God accepted His Son's sacrifice, and that now sinners can be justified without God violating His own law or contradicting His own nature.

The key, of course, is "if we believe" (Rom. 4:24). There are over sixty references to faith or unbelief in Romans. God's saving power is experienced by those who believe in Christ (Rom. 1:16). His righteousness is given to those who believe (Rom. 3:22). We are justified by faith (Rom. 5:1). The object of our faith is Jesus Christ who died for us and rose again.

All of these facts make Abraham's faith that much more wonderful. He did not have a Bible to read; he had only the simple promise of God. He was almost alone as a believer, surrounded by heathen unbelievers. He could not look back at a long record of faith; in fact, he was helping to write that record. Yet Abraham believed God. People today have a complete Bible to read and study. They have a church fellowship and can look back at centuries of faith as recorded in church history and the Bible. Yet many refuse to believe!

Dr. Harry Ironside, for eighteen years pastor of the Moody Church in Chicago, told of visiting a Sunday school class while on vacation. The teacher asked, "How were people saved in Old Testament times?"

After a pause, one man replied, "By keeping the law."

"That's right," said the teacher.

But Dr. Ironside interrupted: "My Bible says that by the deeds of the law shall no flesh be justified."

The teacher was a bit embarrassed, so he said, "Well, does somebody else have an idea?"

Another student replied, "They were saved by bringing sacrifices to God."

"Yes, that's right!" the teacher said, and tried to go on with the lesson.

But Dr. Ironside interrupted, "My Bible says that the blood of bulls and goats cannot take away sin."

By this time the unprepared teacher was sure the visitor knew more about the Bible than he did, so he said, "Well, you tell us how people were saved in the Old Testament!"

And Dr. Ironside explained that they were saved by faith—the same way people are saved today! Twenty-one times in Hebrews 11 you find the same words, "by faith."

If you are a Jew, you are a child of Abraham physically, but are you a child of Abraham spiritually? Abraham is the father of all who believe on Jesus Christ and are justified by faith. If you are a Gentile, you can never be a natural descendant of Abraham, but you can be one of his spiritual descendants. Abraham "believed God and it was counted unto him for righteousness."

QUESTIONS FOR PERSONAL REFLECTION
OR GROUP DISCUSSION

1. What are simple definitions for *justification* and *sanctification*? How would you differentiate between those two words?

2. What are the seven characteristics of justification? Explain each in your own words.

3. How does Abraham's faith illustrate justification?

4. How were the Old Testament believers justified? How are believers justified today?

5. What was the purpose of animal sacrifices in the Old Testament? Why do we no longer need them?

6. What are the key Scriptures that teach justification by faith?

7. What is the link between believing and behaving? How does this affect how you act on a daily, hourly, and minute-by-minute basis?

8. What does it mean that "salvation is free but it is not cheap"? What has it "cost" you?

9. How did God stay true to His own holy nature and law and yet save sinners? How does this make you feel?

10. Why are the words *propitiation*, *redemption*, and *blood* important to understand?

Chapter Four

LIVE LIKE A KING!

(Romans 5)

S ince Romans is a book of logic, it is a book of "therefores." We have the "therefore" of condemnation in Romans 3:20, justification in Romans 5:1, no condemnation in Romans 8:1, and dedication in Romans 12:1. In presenting his case, Paul has proved that the whole world is guilty before God, and that no one can be saved by religious deeds such as keeping the law. He has explained that God's way of salvation has always been "by grace, through faith" (Eph. 2:8–9), and he has used Abraham as his illustration. If a reader of the letter stopped at this point, he would know that he needed to and could be saved.

But there is much more the sinner needs to know about justification by faith. Can he be sure that it will last? How is it possible for God to save a sinner through the death of Christ on the cross? Romans 5 is Paul's explanation of the last two words in Romans 4: "our justification." He explained two basic truths: the blessings of our justification (Rom. 5:1–11), and the basis for our justification (Rom. 5:12–21).

1. THE BLESSINGS OF OUR JUSTIFICATION (5:1–11)

In listing these blessings, Paul accomplished two purposes. First, he told how wonderful it is to be a Christian. Our justification is not simply a guarantee of heaven, as thrilling as that is, but it is also the source of tremendous blessings that we enjoy here and now.

His second purpose was to assure his readers that justification is a lasting thing. His Jewish readers in particular would ask, "Can this spiritual experience last if it does not require obedience to the law? What about the trials and sufferings of life? What about the coming judgment?" When God declared us righteous in Jesus Christ, He gave to us seven spiritual blessings that assure us that we cannot be lost.

(1) Peace with God (v. 1). The unsaved person is at enmity with God (Rom. 5:10; 8:7) because he cannot obey God's law or fulfill God's will. Two verses from Isaiah make the matter clear: "There is no peace, saith the Lord, unto the wicked" (Isa. 48:22); "And the work of righteousness shall be peace" (Isa. 32:17). Condemnation means that God declares us sinners, which is a declaration of war. Justification means that God declares us righteous, which is a declaration of peace, made possible by Christ's death on the cross. "Mercy and truth are met together; righteousness and peace have kissed each other" (Ps. 85:10). "Because the law worketh wrath" (Rom. 4:15), nobody condemned by the law can enjoy peace with God. But when you are justified by faith, you are declared righteous, and the law cannot condemn you or declare war!

(2) Access to God (v. 2a). The Jew was kept from God's presence by the veil in the temple, and the Gentile was kept out by a wall in the temple with a warning on it that any Gentile who went beyond would be killed. But when Jesus died, He tore the veil (Luke 23:45) and broke down the wall (Eph. 2:14). In Christ, believing Jews and Gentiles have access to God (Eph. 2:18; Heb. 10:19–25), and they can draw on the inexhaustible riches of the grace of God (Eph. 1:7; 2:4; 3:8). We stand in grace and not in law. Justification has to do with our standing; sanctification has to do with our state. The child of a king can enter his father's presence no matter how the child looks. The word *access* here means "entrance to the king through the favor of another."

(3) Glorious hope (v. 2b). "Peace with God" takes care of the past: He will no longer hold our sins against us. "Access to God" takes care of the present: We can come to Him at any time for the help we need. "Hope of the glory of God" takes care of the future: One day we shall share in His glory! The word *rejoice* can be translated "boast," not only in Romans 5:2, but also in Romans 5:3 and 11 ("joy"). When we were sinners, there was nothing to boast about (Rom. 3:27), because we fell short of the glory of God (Rom. 3:23). But in Christ, we boast in His righteousness and glory! Paul will amplify this in Romans 8:18–30.

(4) Christian character (vv. 3–4). Justification is no escape from the trials of life. "In the world ye shall have tribulation" (John 16:33). But for the believer, trials work for him and not against him. No amount of suffering can separate us from the Lord (Rom. 8:35–39); instead, trials bring us closer to the Lord and make us more like the Lord. Suffering builds Christian character. The word *experience* in Romans 5:4 means "character that has been proved." The sequence is tribulation—patience—proven character—hope. Our English word *tribulation* comes from a Latin word *tribulum*. In Paul's day, a tribulum was a heavy piece of timber with spikes in it, used for threshing the grain. The tribulum was drawn over the grain and it separated the wheat from the chaff. As we go through tribulations, and depend on God's grace, the trials only purify us and help to get rid of the chaff.

(5) God's love within (vv. 5–8). "Hope deferred maketh the heart sick" (Prov. 13:12). But as we wait for this hope to be fulfilled, the love of God is "poured out into our hearts" (literal translation). Note how the first three of the "fruit of the Spirit" are experienced: love (Rom. 5:5), joy (Rom. 5:2), and peace (Rom. 5:1). Before we were saved, God proved His love by sending

Christ to die for us. Now that we are His children, surely He will love us more. It is the inner experience of this love through the Spirit that sustains us as we go through tribulations.

For many months I visited a young man in a hospital who had almost burned to death. I do not know how many operations and skin grafts he had during those months, or how many specialists visited him. But the thing that sustained him during those difficult months was not the explanations of the doctors but the promises they gave him that he would recover. That was his hope. And the thing that sustained his hope was the love of his family and many friends as they stood by him. The love of God was channeled through them to him. He did recover and today gives glory to God.

Faith (Rom. 5:1), hope (Rom. 5:2), and love (Rom. 5:5) all combine to give the believer patience in the trials of life. And patience makes it possible for the believer to grow in character and become a mature child of God (James 1:1–4).

(6) Salvation from future wrath (vv. 9–10). Paul argued from the lesser to the greater. If God saved us when we were enemies, surely He will keep on saving us now that we are His children. There is a wrath to come, but no true believer will experience it (1 Thess. 1:9–10; 5:8–10). Paul further argued that if Christ's death accomplished so much for us, how much more will He do for us in His life as He intercedes for us in heaven! "Saved by his life" refers to Romans 4:25: "raised again for [on account of] our justification." Because He lives, we are eternally saved (Heb. 7:23–25).

A will is of no effect until the death of the one who wrote it. Then an executor takes over and sees to it that the will is obeyed and the inheritance distributed. But suppose the executor is unscrupulous and wants to get the inheritance for himself? He may figure out many devious ways to circumvent the law and steal the inheritance.

Jesus Christ wrote us into His will, and He wrote the will with His blood. "This cup is the new testament in my blood, which is shed for you" (Luke 22:20). He died so that the will would be in force, but then He arose from the dead and returned to heaven that He might enforce the will Himself and distribute the inheritance. Thus, we are "saved by his life."

(7) **Reconciliation with God (v. 11).** The word *atonement* means "reconciliation, brought back into fellowship with God." The term is mentioned also in Romans 5:10. In Romans 1:18–32, Paul explained how people declared war on God and, because of this, deserved to be condemned eternally. But God did not declare war on humankind. Instead, He sent His Son as the Peacemaker (Eph. 2:11–18), that people might be reconciled to God.

A review of these seven blessings of justification shows how certain our salvation is in Christ. Totally apart from law, and purely by grace, we have a salvation that takes care of the past, the present, and the future. Christ died for us; Christ lives for us; Christ is coming for us! Hallelujah, what a Savior!

2. THE BASIS OF OUR JUSTIFICATION (5:12–21)

How is it possible for God to save sinners in the person of Jesus Christ? We understand that somehow Christ took our place on the cross, but how was such a substitution possible?

Paul answered the question in this section, and these verses are the very heart of the letter. To understand these verses a few general truths about this section need to be understood. First, note the repetition of the little word *one*. It is used eleven times. The key idea here is our identification with Adam and with Christ. Second, note the repetition of the word *reign,* which is used five times. Paul saw two men—Adam and Christ—each of them reigning over a kingdom. Finally, note that the phrase *much more* is repeated five times. This means that in Jesus Christ we have gained much more than we ever lost in Adam!

In short, this section is a contrast of Adam and Christ. Adam was given dominion over the old creation; he sinned, and he lost his kingdom. Because of Adam's sin, all mankind is under condemnation and death. Christ came as the King over a new creation (2 Cor. 5:17). By His obedience on the cross, He brought in righteousness and justification. Christ not only undid all the damage that Adam's sin effected, but He accomplished "much more" by making us the very sons of God. Some of this "much more" Paul has already explained in Romans 5:1–11.

Skeptics sometimes ask, "Was it fair for God to condemn the whole world just because of one man's disobedience?" The answer, of course, is that it was not only fair, but it was also wise and gracious. To begin with, if God had tested each human being individually, the result would have been the same: disobedience. But even more important, by condemning the human race through one man (Adam), God was then able to save the human race through one Man (Jesus Christ)! Each of us is racially united to Adam, so that his deed affects us. (See Heb. 7:9–10 for an example of this racial headship.) The fallen angels cannot be saved because they are not a race. They sinned individually and were judged individually. There can be no representative to take their judgment for them and save them. But because you and I were lost in Adam, our racial head, we can be saved in Christ, the Head of the new creation. God's plan was both gracious and wise.

Our final question must be answered: How do we know that we are racially united to Adam? The answer is in Romans 5:12–14, and the argument runs like this: We know that all men die. But death is the result of disobeying the law. There was no law from Adam to Moses, but men still died. A general result demands a general cause. What is that cause? It can be only one thing: the disobedience of Adam. When Adam sinned, he ultimately died. All of his descendants died (Gen. 5), yet the law had not yet been given. Conclusion: They died because of Adam's sin. "For that all have sinned" (Rom. 5:12) means "all have sinned in Adam's sin." Men do not die because of their own acts of sin; otherwise, babies would not die (Rom. 9:11). Men die because they are united racially to Adam, and "in Adam all die" (1 Cor. 15:22).

Having understood these general truths about the passage, we may now examine the contrasts that Paul gives between Adam and Christ and between Adam's sin and Christ's act of obedience on the cross.

Adam's offense is contrasted with Christ's free gift (v. 15). Because of Adam's trespass, many died; because of Christ's obedience, the grace of God abounds to many bringing life. The word *many* (literally "the many") means the same as "all men" in Romans 5:12 and 18. Note the "much more," for the grace of Christ brings not only physical life, but also spiritual life and abundant life. Christ did conquer death and one day will raise the bodies of all who have died in Christ. If He stopped there, He would only reverse the effects of Adam's sin, but He went on to do "much more." He gives eternal life abundantly to all who trust Him (John 10:10).

The effect of Adam's sin is contrasted with the effect of Christ's obedience (v.16). Adam's sin brought judgment and condemnation, but Christ's work on the cross brings justification. When Adam sinned, he was declared unrighteous and condemned. When a sinner trusts Christ, he is justified—declared righteous in Christ.

The two "reigns" are contrasted (v. 17). Because of Adam's disobedience, death reigned. Read the "book of the generations of Adam" in Genesis 5, and note the solemn repetition of the phrase "and he died." In Romans 5:14, Paul argued that men did not die "from Adam to Moses" for the same reason that Adam died—breaking a revealed law of God—for the law had not yet been given. "The wages of sin is death"

(Rom. 6:23). Because sin was reigning in men's lives (Rom. 5:21), death was also reigning (Rom. 5:14, 17).

But in Jesus Christ we enter a new kingdom: "For the kingdom of God is not meat and drink; but righteousness, and peace, and joy in the Holy Ghost" (Rom. 14:17). "Therefore being justified by faith," we are declared righteous, we have peace with God, and we rejoice in the hope of the glory of God. Note that it is we who reign! "Much more they … shall reign in life by one, Jesus Christ." In Adam we lost our kingship, but in Jesus Christ we reign as kings. And we reign "much more"! Our spiritual reign is far greater than Adam's earthly reign, for we share "abundance of grace and of the gift of righteousness" (Rom. 5:17).

The two "one acts" are contrasted (vv. 18–19). Adam did not have to commit a series of sins. In one act God tested Adam, and he failed. It is termed an "offence" and an act of "disobedience." The word *offense* means "trespass—crossing over the line." God told Adam how far he could go, and Adam decided to go beyond the appointed limit. "Of every tree of the garden thou mayest freely eat: but of the tree of the knowledge of good and evil, thou shalt not eat of it: for in the day that thou eatest thereof, thou shalt surely die" (Gen. 2:16–17).

In contrast to "the offence of one" is "the righteousness of one," meaning the righteous work of Christ on the cross. In Romans 5:19 Paul calls it "the obedience of one" (see Phil. 2:5–12). Christ's sacrifice on the cross not only made possible "justification," but also "justification *of life*" (italics mine). Justification is not merely a legal term that describes our position before God ("just as if I'd never sinned"), but it results in a certain kind of life. "Justification of life" in Romans 5:18 is parallel to "be made righteous" in Romans 5:19. In other words, our justification is the result of a living union with Christ. And this union ought to result in a new kind of life, a righteous life of obedience to

God. Our union with Adam made us sinners; our union with Christ enables us to "reign in life."

Law and grace are contrasted (vv. 20–21). "Then law crept in" (WMS); or, "Then the law came in beside" (literal translation). Grace was not an addition to God's plan; grace was a part of God's plan from the very beginning. God dealt with Adam and Eve in grace; He dealt with the patriarchs in grace; and He dealt with the nation of Israel in grace. He gave the law through Moses, not to replace His grace, but to reveal man's need for grace. Law was temporary, but grace is eternal.

But as the law made man's sins increase, God's grace abounded even more. God's grace was more than adequate to deal with man's sins. Even though sin and death still reign in this world, God's grace is also reigning through the righteousness of Christ. The Christian's body is subject to death and his old nature tempts him to sin, but in Jesus Christ, he can "reign in life" because he is a part of the gracious kingdom of Christ.

An Old Testament story helps us understand the conflict between these two "reigns" in the world today. God rejected Saul as the king of Israel and anointed David. Those who trusted David eventually shared his kingdom of peace and joy. Those who trusted Saul ended in shame and defeat.

Like David, Jesus Christ is God's anointed King. Like Saul, Satan is still free to work in this world and seek to win people's allegiance. Sin and death are reigning in the "old creation" over which Adam was the head, but grace and righteousness are reigning in "the new creation" over which Christ is the Head. And as we yield to Him, we "reign in life."

In Romans 5:14, Adam is called "the figure of him that was to come." Adam was a type, or picture, of Jesus Christ. Adam came from the earth, but Jesus is the Lord from heaven (1 Cor. 15:47). Adam was tested in a garden, surrounded by beauty and love; Jesus was tempted in a wilderness, and He died on a cruel cross surrounded by hatred and ugliness. Adam was a thief, and was cast out of Paradise, but Jesus Christ turned to a thief and said, "Today shalt thou be with me in paradise" (Luke 23:43). The Old Testament is "the book of the generations of Adam" (Gen. 5:1), and it ends with "a curse" (Mal. 4:6). The New Testament is "the book of the generation of Jesus Christ" (Matt. 1:1), and it ends with "no more curse" (Rev. 22:3).

You cannot help being "in Adam," for this came by your first birth, over which you had no control. But you can help staying "in Adam," for you can experience a second birth—a new birth from above—that will put you "in Christ." This is why Jesus said, "Ye must be born again" (John 3:7).

QUESTIONS FOR PERSONAL REFLECTION
OR GROUP DISCUSSION

1. What is the significance of "therefore" as used in Romans 3:20; 5:1; 8:1; and 12:1?

2. Christ died for us "while we were yet sinners" (Rom. 5:8). What does that demonstrate about God?

3. How would you answer the common question, "Is it fair to condemn the whole world just because one man (Adam) disobeyed?"

4. What are the spiritual blessings of our justification? Which of these are most evident in your life today?

5. How are we justified? What is stated in Romans 5:1–21? What does justification mean to you?

6. How does tribulation form Christian character?

7. Who, if anyone, does not have access to God? What does it mean to you to have access to God? How can you better take advantage of this access in your own life?

8. In what way can a believer reign in life?

9. What is the relationship between law, sin, and grace?

Chapter Five

DYING TO LIVE

(Romans 6)

D uring a court session, an attorney will often rise to his feet and say, "Your Honor, I object!" Some of the Roman Christians must have felt like objecting as they heard Paul's letter being read, and Paul seemed to anticipate their thinking. In Romans 6—8 Paul defended his doctrine of justification by faith. He anticipated three objections: (1) "If God's grace abounds when we sin, then let's continue sinning so we might experience more grace" (Rom. 6:1–14); (2) "If we are no longer under the law, then we are free to live as we please" (Rom. 6:15—7:6); and (3) "You have made God's law sinful" (Rom. 7:7–25).

These objections prove that the readers understood neither law nor grace. They were going to extremes: legalism on the one hand and license on the other. So as Paul defended justification he also explained sanctification. He told how we can live lives of victory (Rom. 6), liberty (Rom. 7), and security (Rom. 8). He explained our relationship to the flesh, the law, and the Holy Spirit. In Romans 6, Paul gave three instructions for attaining victory over sin.

1. KNOW (6:1–10)

The repetition of the word *know* in Romans 6:3, 6, and 9 indicates that

Paul wanted us to understand a basic doctrine. Christian living depends on Christian learning; duty is always founded on doctrine. If Satan can keep a Christian ignorant, he can keep him impotent.

The basic truth Paul was teaching is the believer's identification with Christ in death, burial, and resurrection. Just as we are identified with Adam in sin and condemnation, so we are now identified with Christ in righteousness and justification. At Romans 5:12, Paul made a transition from discussing "sins" to discussing "sin"—from the actions to the principle, from the fruit to the root. Jesus Christ not only died for our sins, but He also died unto sin, and we died with Him. Perhaps a chart will explain the contrasts better.

Romans 3:21—5:21	*Romans 6—8*
Substitution: He died for me	Identification: I died with Him
He died *for* my sins	He died *unto* sin
He paid sin's penalty	He broke sin's power
Justification:	Sanctification:
righteousness	righteousness

In other words, justification by faith is not simply a legal matter between me and God; it is a living relationship. It is "a justification which brings life" (Rom. 5:18, literal translation). I am in Christ and identified with Him. Therefore, whatever happened to Christ has happened to me. When He died, I died. When He arose, I arose in Him. I am now seated with Him in the heavenlies (see Eph. 2:1–10; Col. 3:1–3). Because of this living union with Christ, the believer has a totally new relationship to sin.

The believer is dead to sin (vv. 2–5). Paul's illustration is baptism. The Greek word has two basic meanings: (1) a literal meaning—to dip or immerse; and (2) a figurative meaning—to be identified with. An example of the latter would be 1 Corinthians 10:2: "And were all baptized unto Moses in the cloud and in the sea." The nation of Israel was identified with Moses as their leader when they crossed the Red Sea.

It appears that Paul had both the literal and the figurative in mind in this paragraph, for he used the readers' experience of water baptism to remind them of their identification with Christ through the baptism of the Holy Spirit. To be "baptized into Jesus Christ" (Rom. 6:3) is the same as "For by one Spirit are we all baptized into one body" (1 Cor. 12:13). There is a difference between water baptism and the baptism of the Spirit (John 1:33). When a sinner trusts Christ, he is immediately born into the family of God and receives the gift of the Holy Spirit. A good illustration of this is the household of Cornelius when they heard Peter preach (Acts 10:34–48). When these people believed in Christ, they immediately received the Holy Spirit. After that, they were baptized. Peter's words, "Whosoever believeth in him shall receive remission of sins" gave to them the promise that they needed. They believed—and they were saved.

Historians agree that the mode of baptism in the early church was immersion. The believer was "buried" in the water and brought up again as a picture of death, burial, and resurrection. Baptism by immersion (which is the illustration Paul is using in Rom. 6) pictures the believer's identification with Christ in His death, burial, and resurrection. It is an outward symbol of an inward experience. Paul is not saying that their immersion in water put them "into Jesus Christ," for that was accomplished by the Spirit when they believed. Their immersion was a picture of what the Spirit did: The Holy Spirit identified them with Christ in His death, burial, and resurrection.

This means that the believer has a new relationship to sin. He is "dead to sin." "I am crucified with Christ" (Gal. 2:20). If a drunk dies, he can no longer be tempted by alcohol because his body is dead to all physical senses. He cannot see the alcohol, smell it, taste it, or desire it. In Jesus Christ we have died to sin so that we no longer want to "continue in sin." But we are not only dead to sin; we are also alive in Christ. We have been raised from the dead and now walk in the power of His resurrection. We walk in "newness of life" because we share His life. "I am crucified with Christ: nevertheless I live" (Gal. 2:20).

This tremendous spiritual truth is illustrated in the miracle of the resurrection of Lazarus (John 11). When Jesus arrived at Bethany, Lazarus had been in the tomb four days, so there was no question about his death. By the power of His word ("Lazarus, come forth!") Jesus raised His friend from the dead. But when Lazarus appeared at the door of the tomb, he was wrapped in graveclothes. So Jesus commanded, "Loose him, and let him go!" He had been raised to "walk in newness of life." In John 12, Lazarus was seated with Christ at the table, in fellowship with Him. Dead—raised from the dead—set free to walk in newness of life—seated with Christ: All of these facts illustrate the spiritual truths of our identification with Christ as given in Ephesians 2:1–10.

Too many Christians are "betweeners": They live between Egypt and Canaan, saved but never satisfied; or they live between Good Friday and Easter, believing in the cross but not entering into the power and glory of the resurrection. Romans 6:5 indicates that our union with Christ assures our future resurrection should we die. But Romans 6:4 teaches that we share His resurrection power today. "Since, then, you have been raised with Christ, set your hearts on things above ... For you died, and your life is now hidden with Christ in God" (Col. 3:1, 3 NIV).

It is clear, then, that the believer cannot deliberately live in sin since he has a new relationship to sin because of his identification with Christ. The believer has died to the old life; he has been raised to enjoy a new life.

The believer does not want to go back into sin any more than Lazarus wanted to go back into the tomb dressed again in his graveclothes! Then Paul introduced a second fact.

The believer should not serve sin (vv. 6–10). Sin is a terrible master, and it finds a willing servant in the human body. The body is not sinful; the body is neutral. It can be controlled either by sin or by God. But man's fallen nature, which is not changed at conversion, gives sin a beachhead from which it can attack and then control. Paul expressed the problem: "For I know that in me (that is, in my flesh) dwelleth no good thing: for to will is present with me; but how to perform that which is good I find not" (Rom. 7:18).

A tremendous fact is introduced here: The old man (the old ego, self) was crucified with Christ so that the body need not be controlled by sin. The word *destroyed* in Romans 6:6 does not mean annihilated; it means "rendered inactive, made of no effect." The same Greek word is translated "loosed" in Romans 7:2. If a woman's husband dies, she is "loosed" from the law of her husband and is free to marry again. There is a change in relationship. The law is still there, but it has no authority over the woman because her husband is dead.

Sin wants to be our master. It finds a foothold in the old nature, and through the old nature seeks to control the members of the body. But in Jesus Christ, we died to sin, and the old nature was crucified so that the old life is rendered inoperative. Paul was not describing an experience; he was stating a fact. The practical experience was to come later. It is a fact of history that Jesus Christ died on the cross. It is also a fact of history that the believer died with Him, and "he that is dead is freed from sin" (Rom. 6:7). Not "free to sin" as Paul's accusers falsely stated, but "freed from sin."

Sin and death have no dominion over Christ. We are "in Christ";

therefore, sin and death have no dominion over us. Jesus Christ not only died "for sin," but He also died "unto sin." That is, He not only paid the penalty for sin, but He broke the power of sin. This idea of dominion takes us back to Romans 5:12–21, where Paul dealt with the "reigns" of sin, death, and grace. Through Christ we "reign in life" (Rom. 5:17) so that sin no longer controls our lives.

The big question now is, "I believe the facts of history, but how do I make this work in daily experience?" This leads to Paul's second instruction.

2. Reckon (6:11)

In some parts of the United States, "to reckon" means "to think" or "to guess." "I reckon" is also the equivalent of "I suppose." But none of these popular meanings can apply to this verse. The word *reckon* is a translation of a Greek word that is used forty-one times in the New Testament—nineteen times in Romans alone. It appears in Romans 4, where it is translated as "count, reckon, impute." It means "to take into account, to calculate, to estimate." The word *impute*—"to put to one's account"—is perhaps the best translation.

To *reckon* also means "to put to one's account." It simply means to believe that what God says in His Word is really true in your life.

Paul didn't tell his readers to *feel* as if they were dead to sin, or even to *understand* it fully, but to *act* on God's Word and claim it for themselves. Reckoning is a matter of faith that issues in action. It is like endorsing a check: If we really believe that the money is in the checking account, we will sign our name and collect the money. Reckoning is not claiming a promise but acting on a fact. God does not command us to become dead to sin. He tells us that we *are* dead to sin and alive unto God and then commands us to act on it. Even if we do not act on it, the facts are still true.

Paul's first instruction ("know") centered in the *mind,* and this second instruction ("reckon") focuses on the *heart.* His third instruction touches the *will.*

3. YIELD (6:12–23)

The word *yield* is found five times in this section (Rom. 6:13, 16, 19) and means "to place at one's disposal, to present, to offer as a sacrifice." According to Romans 12:1, the believer's body should be presented to the Lord as "a living sacrifice" for His glory. The Old Testament sacrifices were dead sacrifices. The Lord may ask some of us to die for Him, but He asks all of us to *live* for Him.

How we are to yield (vv. 12–13). This is an act of the will based on the knowledge we have of what Christ has done for us. It is an intelligent act—not the impulsive decision of the moment based on some emotional stirring. It is important to notice the tenses of the verbs in these verses. A literal translation is "Do not constantly allow sin to reign in your mortal body so that you are constantly obeying its lusts. Neither constantly yield your members of your body as weapons [or tools] of unrighteousness to sin; but once and for all yield yourselves to God." That once-and-for-all surrender is described in Romans 12:1.

There must be in the believer's life that final and complete surrender of the body to Jesus Christ. This does not mean there will be no further steps of surrender, because there will be. The longer we walk with Christ, the deeper the fellowship must become. But there can be no subsequent steps without that first step. The tense of the verb in Romans 12:1 corresponds with that in Romans 6:13—a once-and-for-all yielding to the Lord. To be sure, we daily surrender afresh to Him, but even that is based on a final and complete surrender.

Why does the Lord want your body? To begin with, the believer's body is God's temple, and He wants to use it for His glory (1 Cor. 6:19–20; Phil. 1:20–21). But Paul wrote that the body is also God's tool and God's weapon (Rom. 6:13). God wants to use the members of the body as tools for building His kingdom and weapons for fighting His enemies.

The Bible tells of people who permitted God to take and use their bodies for the fulfilling of His purposes. God used the rod in Moses' hand and conquered Egypt. He used the sling in David's hand to defeat the Philistines. He used the mouths and tongues of the prophets. Paul's dedicated feet carried him from city to city as he proclaimed the gospel. The apostle John's eyes saw visions of the future, his ears heard God's message, and his fingers wrote it all down in a book that we can read.

But you can also read in the Bible accounts of the members of the body being used for sinful purposes. David's eyes looked on his neighbor's wife; his mind plotted a wicked scheme; his hand signed a cowardly order for the woman's husband to be killed. As you read Psalm 51, you see that his whole body was affected by sin: his eyes (Ps. 51:3), mind (Ps. 51:6), ears (Ps. 51:8), heart (Ps. 51:10), and lips and mouth (Ps. 51:14–15). No wonder he prayed for a *thorough* cleansing (Ps. 51:2)!

Why we are to yield (vv. 14–23). Three words summarize the reasons for our yielding: *favor* (Rom. 6:14–15), *freedom* (Rom. 6:16–20), and *fruit* (Rom. 6:21–23).

Favor (vv. 14–15). It is because of God's grace that we yield ourselves to Him. Paul has proved that we are not saved by the law and that we do not live under the law. The fact that we are saved by grace does not give us an excuse to sin, but it does give us a reason to obey. Sin and law go together. "The sting of death is sin; and the strength of sin is the law" (1 Cor. 15:56). Since we are not under law, but under grace, sin is robbed of its strength.

Freedom (vv. 16–20). The illustration of the master and servant is obvious. Whatever you yield to becomes your master. Before you were saved, you were the slave of sin. Now that you belong to Christ, you are freed from that old slavery and made the servant of Christ. Romans 6:19 suggests that the Christian ought to be as enthusiastic in yielding to the Lord as he was in yielding to sin. A friend once said to me, "I want to be as good a saint as I was a sinner!" I knew what he meant because in his unconverted days he was almost "the chief of sinners."

The unsaved person is free—free *from* righteousness (Rom. 6:20). But his bondage to sin only leads him deeper into slavery so that it becomes harder and harder to do what is right. The Prodigal Son is an example of this (Luke 15:11–24). When he was at home, he decided he wanted his freedom, so he left home to find himself and enjoy himself. But his rebellion only led him deeper into slavery. He was the slave of wrong desires, then the slave of wrong deeds, and finally he became a literal slave when he took care of the pigs. He wanted to find himself, but he lost himself! What he thought was freedom turned out to be the worst kind of slavery. It was only when he returned home and *yielded to his father* that he found true freedom.

Fruit (vv. 21–23). If you serve a master, you can expect to receive wages. Sin pays wages—death! God also pays wages—holiness and everlasting life. In the old life, we produced fruit that made us ashamed. In the new life in Christ, we produce fruit that glorifies God and brings joy to our lives. We usually apply Romans 6:23 to the lost, and certainly it does apply, but it also has a warning for the saved. (After all, it was written to Christians.) "There is a sin not unto death" (1 John 5:17). "For this reason many among you are weak and sick, and a number sleep" (1 Cor. 11:30 NASB). Samson, for example, would not yield himself to God, but preferred to yield to the lusts of the flesh, and the result was death (Judg. 16). If the believer refuses to surrender his body to the Lord but uses its members for sinful purposes, then he is in danger of being disciplined by the Father, and this could mean death. (See Heb. 12:5–11; note the end of verse 9 in particular.)

These three instructions need to be heeded each day that we live. *Know* that you have been crucified with Christ and are dead to sin. *Reckon* this fact to be true in your own life. *Yield* your body to the Lord to be used for His glory.

Now that you *know* these truths, *reckon* them to be true in your life, and then *yield* yourself to God.

QUESTIONS FOR PERSONAL REFLECTION
OR GROUP DISCUSSION

1. What are three objections to the doctrine of justification by faith? How would you answer each of these objections?

2. Why is justification considered a living relationship?

3. What does Wiersbe mean when he describes some Christians as "betweeners"?

4. What is the meaning of baptism?

5. What should be the believer's relationship to sin? What does this look like in your own life?

6. How would you distinguish between the words *know*, *reckon*, and *yield* as ways to attain victory over sin?

7. How can we yield ourselves or present ourselves to God?

8. Why does God want our bodies? How might knowing this change how you live your daily life?

9. What might happen if we refuse to surrender our bodies to the Lord?

10. How are the words *favor* (vv. 14–15), *freedom* (vv. 16–20), and *fruit* (vv. 21–23) related to yielding?

Chapter Six

CHRISTIANS AND THE LAW

(Romans 7)

Something in human nature makes us want to go to extremes, a weakness from which Christians are not wholly free. "Since we are saved by grace," some argue, "we are free to live as we please," which is the extreme of *license*.

"But we cannot ignore God's law," others argue. "We are saved by grace, to be sure; but we must live under law if we are to please God." This is the extreme expression of *legalism*.

Paul answered the first group in Romans 6; the second group he answers in Romans 7. The word *law* is used twenty-three times in this chapter. In Romans 6, Paul told us how to stop doing bad things; in Romans 7 he tells how *not* to do good things. "You were not justified by keeping the law," he argued, "and you cannot be sanctified by keeping the law."

Every growing Christian understands the experience of Romans 6 and 7. Once we learn how to "know, reckon, and yield," we start getting victory over the habits of the flesh, and we feel we are becoming more spiritual. We set high standards and ideals for ourselves and for a while seem to attain them.

Then everything collapses! We start to see deeper into our own hearts, and we discover sins that we did not know were there. God's holy law takes on a new power, and we wonder if we can ever do anything good. Without realizing it, we have moved into legalism and have learned the truth about sin, the law, and ourselves.

What really is legalism? It is the belief that I can become holy and please God by obeying laws. It is measuring spirituality by a list of dos and don'ts. The weakness of legalism is that it sees *sins* (plural) but not *sin* (the root of the trouble). It judges by the outward and not the inward. Furthermore, the legalist fails to understand the real purpose of God's law and the relationship between law and grace.

In my pastoral experience, I have counseled many people who have suffered severe emotional and spiritual damage because they have tried to live holy lives on the basis of a high standard. I have seen the consequences of these attempts: Either the person becomes a pretender, or he suffers a complete collapse and abandons his desires for godly living. I have seen too that many legalists are extremely hard on other people—critical, unloving, unforgiving. Paul wanted to spare his readers this difficult and dangerous experience. In Romans 7, he discussed three topics, which, if understood and applied, will deliver us from legalism.

1. THE AUTHORITY OF THE LAW (7:1–6)

These verses actually continue the discussion that Paul began in Romans 6:15, answering the question, "Shall we sin because we are not under the law but under grace?" He used the illustration of a master and servant to explain how the Christian should yield himself to God. In this passage he used the illustration of a husband and wife to show that the believer has a new relationship to the law because of his union with Jesus Christ.

The illustration is a simple one, but it has a profound application.

When a man and woman marry, they are united for life. Marriage is a physical union ("They shall be one flesh" Gen. 2:24) and can only be broken by a physical cause. One such cause is *death*. (Matt. 5:31–34; 19:1–12 indicate that unfaithfulness also breaks the marriage bond, but Paul does not bring this up. He is not discussing marriage and divorce; he is using marriage to illustrate a point.)

As long as they live, the husband and wife are under the authority of the law of marriage. If the woman leaves the man and marries another man, she commits adultery. But if the husband dies, she is free to remarry because she is no longer a wife. It is death that has broken the marriage relationship and set her free.

Paul's application in Romans 7:4–6 clinches the argument. He states two marvelous facts that explain the believer's relationship to the law.

(1) We died to the law (vv. 4–5). It appears that Paul has confused his illustration, but he has not. When we were unsaved ("in the flesh," Rom. 7:5), we were under the authority of God's law. We were condemned by that law. When we trusted Christ and were united to Him, *we died to the law* just as we died to the flesh (Rom. 6:1–10). The law did not die; *we* died.

But in Paul's illustration from marriage, it was the *husband* who died and the wife who married again. If you and I are represented by the wife, and the law is represented by the husband, then the application does not follow the illustration. If the wife died in the illustration, the only way she could marry again would be to come back from the dead. But that is exactly what Paul wants to teach. When we trusted Christ, we died to the law; but in Christ, we arose from the dead and now are "married" (united) to Christ to live a new kind of life.

The law did not die, because God's law still rules over people. We died to the law, and it no longer has dominion over us. But we are not "lawless"; we are united to Christ, sharing His life, and thus walking "in newness of life." Romans 8:4 climaxes the argument: "That the righteousness of the law might be fulfilled in us, who walk not after the flesh but after the Spirit." In the old life of sin, we brought forth fruit "unto death," but in the new life of grace, we "bring forth fruit unto God." To be "dead to the law" does not mean that we lead lawless lives. It simply means that the *motivation* and *dynamic* of our lives does not come from the law: It comes from God's grace through our union with Christ.

(2) **We are delivered from law (v. 6).** This is the logical conclusion: The law cannot exercise authority over a dead person. The Authorized Version reads as though the law died, but Paul wrote, "We having died to that wherein we were held." Death means deliverance (note Rom. 6:9–10). But we were delivered that we might serve. The Christian life is not one of independence and rebellion. We died to the law that we might be "married to Christ." We were delivered from the law that we might serve Christ. This truth refutes the false accusation that Paul taught lawlessness.

What is different about Christian service as opposed to our old life of sin? To begin with, the Holy Spirit of God energizes us as we seek to obey and serve the Lord. (The word *spirit* ought to be capitalized in Romans 7:6—"newness of Spirit.") Under law, no enablement was given. God's commandments were written on stones and read to the people. But under grace, God's Word is written in our hearts (2 Cor. 3:1–3). We "walk in newness of life" (Rom. 6:4) and serve "in newness of Spirit." The believer, then, is no longer under the authority of the law.

2. THE MINISTRY OF THE LAW (7:7–13)

Paul's objectors were ready: "What good is the law if we don't need it anymore? Why, a teaching such as yours turns the law into sin!" In answering that objection, Paul explained the ministries of the law, ministries that function even today.

The law reveals sin (v. 7). "By the law is the knowledge of sin" (Rom. 3:20). "Where no law is, there is no transgression" (Rom. 4:15). The law is a mirror that reveals the inner man and shows us how dirty we are (James 1:22–25). Note that Paul did not use murder, stealing, or adultery in his discussion; he uses *coveting*. This is the last of the Ten Commandments, and it differs from the other nine in that it is an inward attitude, not an outward action. Covetousness leads to the breaking of the other commandments. It is an insidious sin that most people never recognize in their own lives, but God's law reveals it.

The rich ruler in Mark 10:17–27 is a good example of the use of the law to reveal sin and show a man his need for a Savior. The young man was very moral outwardly, but he had never faced the sins within. Jesus did not tell him about the law because the law would save him; He told him about the law because the young man did not realize his own sinfulness. True, he had never committed adultery, robbed anyone, given false witness, or dishonored his parents, but what about covetousness? When Jesus told him to sell his goods and give to the poor, the man went away in great sorrow. The commandment "Thou shalt not covet" had revealed to him what a sinner he really was! Instead of admitting his sin, he rejected Christ and went away unconverted.

The law arouses sin (vv. 8–9). Since Paul was a devout Pharisee, seeking to obey the law before his conversion, it is easier to understand these verses. (Read Phil. 3:1–11 and Gal. 1 for other autobiographical data on Paul's relationship to the law in his unconverted days.) Keep in mind too that "the strength of sin is the law" (1 Cor. 15:56). Since we have a sinful nature, the law is bound to arouse that nature the way a magnet draws steel.

Something in human nature wants to rebel whenever a law is given. I was standing in Lincoln Park in Chicago, looking at the newly painted benches, and I noticed a sign on each bench: Do Not Touch. As I watched,

I saw numbers of people deliberately reach out and touch the wet paint! Why? Because the sign told them not to! Instruct a child not to go near the water, and that is the very thing he will do. Why? "Because the carnal mind is enmity against God: for it is not subject to the law of God, neither indeed can be" (Rom. 8:7).

Believers who try to live by rules and regulations discover that their legalistic system only arouses more sin and creates more problems. The churches in Galatia were very legalistic, and they experienced all kinds of trouble. "But if ye bite and devour one another, take heed that ye be not consumed one of another" (Gal. 5:15). Their legalism did not make them more spiritual; it made them more sinful. Why? Because the law arouses sin in our nature.

The law kills (vv. 10–11). "For if there had been a law given which could have given life, verily righteousness should have been by the law" (Gal. 3:21). But the law cannot give life: It can only show the sinner that he is guilty and condemned. This explains why legalistic Christians and churches do not grow and bear spiritual fruit. They are living by law, and the law always kills. Few things are more dead than an orthodox church that is proud of its "high standards" and tries to live up to them in its own energy. Often the members of such a church start to judge and condemn one another, and the sad result is a church fight and then a church split that leaves members—or former members—angry and bitter.

As the new Christian grows, he comes into contact with various philosophies of the Christian life. He can read books, attend seminars, listen to tapes, and get a great deal of information. If he is not careful, he will start following a human leader and accept his teachings as law. This practice is a very subtle form of legalism, and it kills spiritual growth. No human teacher can take the place of Christ; no book can take the place of the Bible. Men can give us information, but only the Spirit can give us illumination and help us understand spiritual truths. The Spirit enlightens us and enables us; no human leader can do that.

The law shows the sinfulness of sin (vv. 12–13). Unsaved people know that there is such a thing as sin, but they do not realize the sinfulness of sin. Many Christians do not realize the true nature of sin. We excuse our sins with words like "mistakes" or "weaknesses," but God condemns our sins and tries to get us to see that they are "exceedingly sinful." Until we realize how wicked sin really is, we will never want to oppose it and live in victory.

Paul's argument here is tremendous: (1) the law is not sinful—it is holy, just, and good; (2) but the law reveals sin, arouses sin, and then uses sin to slay us; if something as good as the law accomplishes these results, then something is radically wrong somewhere; (3) conclusion: see how sinful sin is when it can use something good like the law to produce such tragic results. Sin is indeed "exceedingly sinful." The problem is not with the law; the problem is with my sinful nature. This prepares the way for the third topic in this chapter.

3. THE INABILITY OF THE LAW (7:14–25)

Having explained what the law is supposed to do, Paul now explains what the law cannot do.

The law cannot change you (v. 14). The character of the law is described in four words: holy, just, good, and spiritual. That the law is holy and just, nobody can deny, because it came from the holy God who is perfectly just in all that He says and does. The law is good. It reveals God's holiness to us and helps us to see our need for a Savior.

What does it mean that the law is "spiritual"? It means that the law deals with the inner man, the spiritual part of man, as well as with the outer actions. In the original giving of the law in Exodus, the emphasis was on the outward actions. But when Moses restated the law in Deuteronomy, he emphasized the inner quality of the law as it relates to man's heart. This spiritual emphasis is stated clearly in Deuteronomy 10:12–13. The repetition of the word *love* in Deuteronomy also shows that the deeper interpretation of the law relates to the inner man (Deut. 4:37; 6:4–6; 10:12; 11:1; 30:6, 16, 20).

Our nature is carnal (fleshly), but the law's nature is spiritual. This explains why the old nature responds as it does to the law. It has well been said, "The old nature knows no law, the new nature needs no law." The law cannot transform the old nature; it can only reveal how sinful that old nature is. The believer who tries to live under law will only *activate* the old nature; he will not eradicate it.

The law cannot enable you to do good (vv. 15–21). Three times in this passage Paul stated that sin dwells in us (Rom. 7:17, 18, 20). He was referring, of course, to the old nature. It is also true that the Holy Spirit dwells in us; and in Romans 8, Paul explained how the Spirit of God enables us to live in victory, something the law cannot help us do.

The many pronouns in this section indicate that the writer is having a problem with *self.* This is not to say that the Christian is a split personality, because he is not. Salvation makes a man whole. But it does indicate that the believer's mind, will, and body can be controlled either by the old nature or the new nature, either by the flesh or the Spirit. The statements here indicate that the believer has two serious problems: (1) he cannot do the good he wants to do, and (2) he does the evil that he does not want to do.

Does this mean that Paul could not stop himself from breaking God's law—that he was a liar and thief and murderer? Of course not! Paul was saying that of *himself* he could not obey God's law, and that even when he did, evil was still present with him. No matter what he did, his deeds were tainted by sin. Even after he had done his best, he had to admit that he was "an unprofitable servant" (Luke 17:10). "So I find this law at work: when I want to do good, evil is right there with me" (Rom. 7:21 NIV). This, of course, is a different problem from that in Romans 6. The problem there was, "How can I stop doing bad things?" while the problem here is, "How can I ever do anything good?"

The legalist says, "Obey the law and you will do good and live a good life." But the law only reveals and arouses sin, showing how sinful it is! It is impossible for me to obey the law because I have a sinful nature that rebels against the law. Even if I think I have done good, I know that evil is present. The law is good, but by nature, I am bad! So the legalist is wrong: The law cannot enable us to do good.

The law cannot set you free (vv. 21–25). The believer has an old nature that wants to keep him in bondage; "I will get free from these old sins!" the Christian says to himself. "I determine here and now that I will not do this any longer." What happens? He exerts all his willpower and energy, and for a time succeeds, but then when he least expects it, he falls again. Why? Because he tried to overcome his old nature with law, and the law cannot deliver us from the old nature. When you move under the law, you are only making the old nature stronger because "the strength of sin is the law" (1 Cor. 15:56). Instead of being a dynamo that gives us power to overcome, the law is a magnet that draws out of us all kinds of sin and corruption. The inward man may delight in the law of God (Ps. 119:35), but the old nature delights in breaking the law of God. No wonder the believer under law becomes tired and discouraged, and eventually gives up! He is a captive, and his condition is "wretched." (The Greek word indicates a person who is exhausted after a battle.) What could be more wretched than exerting all your energy to try to live a good life, only to discover that the best you do is still not good enough!

Is there any deliverance? Of course! I thank God that there is Someone who shall deliver me—Jesus Christ our Lord! Because the believer is united to Christ, he is dead to the law and no longer under its authority. But he is alive to God and able to draw on the power of the Holy Spirit. The explanation of this victory is given in Romans 8.

The final sentence in the chapter does not teach that the believer lives a divided life: sinning with his flesh but serving God with his mind. This would mean that his body was being used in two different ways *at the same time,* and this is impossible. The believer realizes that there is a struggle within him between the flesh and the Spirit (Gal. 5:16–18), but he knows that one or the other must be in control.

By "the mind" Paul meant "the inward man" (Rom. 7:22) as opposed to "the flesh" (Rom. 7:18). He amplified this thought in Romans 8:5–8. The old nature cannot do anything good. Everything the Bible says about the old nature is negative: "no good thing" (Rom. 7:18); "the flesh profiteth nothing" (John 6:63); "no confidence in the flesh" (Phil. 3:3). If we depend on the energy of the flesh, we cannot serve God, please God, or do any good thing. But if we yield to the Holy Spirit, then we have the power needed to obey His will. The flesh will never serve the law of God because the flesh is at war with God. But the Spirit can only obey the law of God! Therefore, the secret of doing good is to yield to the Holy Spirit.

Paul hinted at this in the early verses of this chapter when he wrote, "That we should bring forth fruit unto God" (Rom. 7:4). Just as we are dead to the old nature, so we are dead to the law. But we are united to Christ and alive in Christ, and therefore can bring forth fruit unto God. It is our union with Christ that enables us to serve God acceptably. "For it is God which worketh in you, both to will and to do of his good pleasure" (Phil. 2:13). That solved Paul's problem in Romans 7:18: "For to will is present with me; but how to perform that which is good I find not."

The old nature knows no law and the new nature needs no law. Legalism makes a believer wretched because it grieves the new nature and aggravates the old nature. The legalist becomes a Pharisee whose outward actions are acceptable, but whose inward attitudes are despicable. No wonder Jesus called them "whited sepulchres, which indeed appear beautiful outward, but are within full of dead men's bones, and of all uncleanness" (Matt. 23:27). How wretched can you get!

The best is yet to come! Romans 8 explains the work of the Holy Spirit in overcoming the bad and producing the good.

QUESTIONS FOR PERSONAL REFLECTION
OR GROUP DISCUSSION

1. What is the authority of the law (7:1–6)?

2. How did Paul use the illustration of marriage to help us understand our relation to the law?

3. What is different in us as believers that wasn't there when we were under the law? What difference has this made in your life?

4. What are at least four ways the law ministers to us today (7:7–13)?

5. Why do you think Paul may have used the commandment "you shall not covet" as an example of lawbreaking? What are some laws you struggle with personally?

6. Why is the law unable to help us (7:14–25)?

7. What does it mean to be legalistic? Where can you improve on this in your own life?

8. What effect does legalism have on the Christian life? How can we be delivered from legalism?

9. Why is it impossible to obey the law and live a good life? What is the secret of doing good? Why?

10. What is the role of the Holy Spirit today?

Chapter Seven

FREEDOM AND FULFILLMENT

(Romans 8)

On January 6, 1941, President Franklin Delano Roosevelt addressed Congress on the state of the war in Europe. Much of what he said that day has been forgotten. But at the close of his address, he said that he looked forward "to a world founded upon four essential human freedoms." He named them: freedom of speech, freedom of worship, freedom from want, and freedom from fear. These words are still remembered, even though their ideals have not yet been realized everywhere in the world.

Romans 8 is the Christian's "Declaration of Freedom," for in it Paul declares the four spiritual freedoms we enjoy because of our union with Jesus Christ. A study of this chapter shows the emphasis on the Holy Spirit, who is mentioned nineteen times. "Where the Spirit of the Lord is, there is liberty" (2 Cor. 3:17).

1. FREEDOM FROM JUDGMENT—NO CONDEMNATION (8:1–4)

Romans 3:20 shows the "therefore" of condemnation, but Romans 8:1 gives the "therefore" of *no* condemnation—a tremendous truth and the conclusion of a marvelous argument. (The words "who walk not ... etc." do not belong here according to the best manuscripts. There are no conditions for us to meet.) The basis for this wonderful assurance is the phrase "in Christ Jesus." In Adam, we were condemned. In Christ, there is no condemnation!

The verse does not say "no mistakes" or "no failures," or even "no sins." Christians *do* fail and make mistakes, and they do sin. Abraham lied about his wife; David committed adultery; Peter tried to kill a man with his sword. To be sure, they suffered consequences because of their sins, but they did not suffer condemnation.

The law condemns, but the believer has a new relationship to the law, and therefore he cannot be condemned. Paul made three statements about the believer and the law, and together they add up to *no condemnation.*

(1) The law cannot claim you (v. 2). You have been made free from the law of sin and death. You now have life in the Spirit. You have moved into a whole new sphere of life in Christ. "The law of sin and death" is what Paul described in Romans 7:7–25. "The law of the Spirit of life" is described in Romans 8. The law no longer has any jurisdiction over you: You are dead to the law (Rom. 7:4) and free from the law (Rom. 8:2).

(2) The law cannot condemn you (v. 3). Why? Because Christ has already suffered that condemnation for you on the cross. The law could not save; it can only condemn. But God sent His Son to save us and do what the law could not do. Jesus did not come as an angel; He came as a man. He did not come "in sinful flesh," for that would have made Him a sinner. He came *in the likeness* of sinful flesh, as a man. He bore our sins in His body on the cross.

The "law of double jeopardy" states that a person cannot be tried twice for the same crime. Since Jesus Christ paid the penalty for your sins, and since you are "in Christ," God will not condemn you.

(3) The law cannot control you (v. 4). The believer lives a righteous life, not in the power of the law, but in the power of the Holy Spirit. The law does not have the power to produce holiness; it can only reveal and condemn sin. But the indwelling Holy Spirit enables you to walk in obedience to God's will. The righteousness that God demands in His law is fulfilled in you through the Spirit's power. In the Holy Spirit, you have life and liberty (Rom. 8:2) and the pursuit of happiness (Rom. 8:4).

The legalist tries to obey God in his own strength and fails to measure up to the righteousness that God demands. The Spirit-led Christian, as he yields to the Lord, experiences the sanctifying work of the Spirit in his life. "For it is God which worketh in you, both to will and to do of his good pleasure" (Phil. 2:13). It is this fact that leads to the second freedom we enjoy as Christians.

2. FREEDOM FROM DEFEAT—NO OBLIGATION (8:5–17)

"Therefore, brethren, we are debtors, not to the flesh, to live after the flesh" (Rom. 8:12). There is no obligation to the old nature. The believer can live in victory. In this section, Paul described life on three different levels, and he encouraged his readers to live on the highest level.

(1) **"You have not the Spirit" (vv. 5–8).** Paul is not describing two kinds of Christians, one carnal and one spiritual. He is contrasting the saved and the unsaved. There are four contrasts.

In the flesh—in the Spirit (v. 5). The unsaved person does not have the Spirit of God (Rom. 8:9) and lives *in* the flesh and *for* the flesh. His mind is centered on the things that satisfy the flesh. But the Christian has the Spirit of God within and lives in an entirely new and different sphere. His mind is fixed on the things of the Spirit. This does not mean that the unsaved person never does anything good, or that the believer never does anything bad. It means that the bent of their lives is different. One lives for the flesh, the other lives for the Spirit.

Death—life (v. 6). The unsaved person is alive physically, but dead spiritually. The inner man is dead toward God and does not respond to the things of the Spirit. He may be moral, and even religious, but he lacks spiritual life. He needs "the Spirit of life in Christ Jesus" (Rom. 8:2).

War with God—peace with God (vv. 6–7). In our study of Romans 7, we have seen that the old nature rebels against God and will not submit to God's law. Those who have trusted Christ enjoy "peace with God" (Rom. 5:1), while the unsaved are at war with God. "'There is no peace,' saith the Lord, 'unto the wicked'" (Isa. 48:22).

Pleasing self—pleasing God (v. 8). To be "in the flesh" means to be lost, outside Christ. The unsaved person lives to please himself and rarely if ever thinks about pleasing God. The root of sin is selfishness—"I will" and not "Thy will."

To be unsaved and not have the Spirit is the lowest level of life. But a person need not stay on that level. By faith in Christ he can move to the second level.

"You have the Spirit" (vv. 9–11). "But ye are not in the flesh, but in the Spirit, if so be that the Spirit of God dwell in you" (Rom. 8:9). The evidence of conversion is the presence of the Holy Spirit within, witnessing that you are a child of God (Rom. 8:16). Your body becomes the very temple of the Holy Spirit (1 Cor. 6:19–20). Even though the body is destined to die because of sin (unless, of course, the Lord returns), the Spirit gives life to that body today so that we may serve God. If we should die, the body will one day be raised from the dead, because the Holy Spirit has sealed each believer (Eph. 1:13–14).

What a difference it makes in your body when the Holy Spirit lives within. You experience new life, and even your physical faculties take on a new dimension of experience. When evangelist D. L. Moody described his conversion experience, he said: "I was in a new world. The next morning the sun shone brighter and the birds sang sweeter … the old elms waved their branches for joy, and all nature was at peace." Life in Christ is abundant life.

But there is a third level of experience for which the other two are preparation.

(3) "The Spirit has you!" (vv. 12–17). It is not enough for us to have the Spirit; the Spirit must have us! Only then can He share with us the abundant, victorious life that can be ours in Christ. We have no obligation to the flesh, because the flesh has only brought trouble into our lives. We do have an obligation to the Holy Spirit, for it is the Spirit who convicted us, revealed Christ to us, and imparted eternal life to us when we trusted Christ. Because He is "the Spirit of Life," He can empower us to obey Christ, and He can enable us to be more like Christ.

But He is also the Spirit of death. He can enable us to "put to death" (mortify) the sinful deeds of the body. As we yield the members of our body to the Spirit (Rom. 6:12–17), He applies to us and in us the death and resurrection of Christ. He puts to death the things of the flesh, and He reproduces the things of the Spirit.

The Holy Spirit is also "the Spirit of adoption" (Rom. 8:14–17). The word *adoption* in the New Testament means "being placed as an adult son." We come into God's family by birth. But the instant we are born into the family, God adopts us and gives us the position of an adult son. A baby cannot walk, speak, make decisions, or draw on the family wealth. But the believer can do all of these the instant he is born again.

He can walk and be "led by the Spirit" (Rom. 8:14). The verb here means "willingly led." We yield to the Spirit, and He guides us by His Word day by day. We are not under bondage to law and afraid to act. We have the liberty of the Spirit and are free to follow Christ. The believer can also speak: "We cry, Abba, Father" (Rom. 8:15). Would it not be amazing if a newborn baby looked up and greeted his father! First, the Spirit says, "Abba, Father" to us (Gal. 4:6), and then we say it to God. ("Abba" means "papa"—a term of endearment.)

A baby cannot sign checks, but the child of God by faith can draw on his spiritual wealth because he is an heir of God and a joint-heir with Christ (Rom. 8:17). The Spirit teaches us from the Word, and then we receive God's wealth by faith. What a thrilling thing it is to have "the Spirit of adoption" at work in our lives!

There is no need for the believer to be defeated. He can yield his body to the Spirit and by faith overcome the old nature. The Spirit of life will empower him. The Spirit of death will enable him to overcome the flesh. And the Spirit of adoption will enrich him and lead him into the will of God.

3. Freedom from Discouragement—No Frustration (8:18–30)

In this section Paul dealt with the very real problem of suffering and pain. Perhaps the best way to understand this section is to note the three "groans" that are discussed.

(1) Creation groans (vv. 18–22). When God finished His creation, it was a good creation (Gen. 1:31), but today it is a groaning creation. There is suffering and death; there is pain, all of which is, of course, the result of Adam's sin. It is not the fault of creation. Note the words that Paul used to describe the plight of creation: suffering (Rom. 8:18), vanity (Rom. 8:20), bondage (Rom. 8:21), decay (Rom. 8:21 NIV), and pain (Rom. 8:22). However, this groaning is not a useless thing: Paul compared it to a woman in travail. There is pain, but the pain will end when the child is delivered. One day creation will be delivered, and the groaning creation will become a glorious creation. The believer does not focus on today's sufferings; she looks forward to tomorrow's glory (Rom. 8:18; 2 Cor. 4:15–18). Today's groaning bondage will be exchanged for tomorrow's glorious liberty!

(2) We believers groan (vv. 23–25). The reason we groan is because we have experienced "the firstfruits of the Spirit," a foretaste of the glory to come. Just as the nation of Israel tasted the firstfruits of Canaan when the spies returned (Num. 13:23–27), so we Christians have tasted of the blessings of heaven through the ministry of the Spirit. This makes us want to see the Lord, receive a new body, and live with Him and serve Him forever. We are waiting for "the adoption," which is the redemption of the body when Christ returns (Phil. 3:20–21). This is the thrilling climax to "the adoption" that took place at conversion when "the Spirit of adoption" gave us an adult standing in God's family. When Christ returns, we shall enter into our full inheritance.

Meanwhile, we wait and hope. "For we are saved by that hope" (Rom. 8:24, literal translation). What hope? "That blessed hope, and the glorious appearing of the great God and our Saviour Jesus Christ" (Titus 2:13). The best is yet to come! The believer does not get frustrated as he sees and experiences suffering and pain in this world. He knows that the temporary suffering will one day give way to eternal glory.

(3) The Holy Spirit groans (vv. 25–30). God is concerned about the trials of His people. When He was ministering on earth, Jesus groaned when He saw what sin was doing to mankind (Mark 7:34; John 11:33, 38). Today the Holy Spirit groans with us and feels the burdens of our weaknesses and suffering. But the Spirit does more than groan. He prays for us in His groaning so that we might be led into the will of God. We do not always know God's will. We do not always know how to pray, but the Spirit intercedes so that we might live in the will of God in spite of suffering. The Spirit "shares the burden."

The believer never need faint in times of suffering and trial because he knows that God is at work in the world (Rom. 8:28), and that He has a perfect plan (Rom. 8:29). God has two purposes in that plan: our good and His glory. Ultimately, He will make us like Jesus Christ. Best of all, God's plan is going to succeed. It started in eternity past when He chose us in Christ (Eph. 1:4–5). He predetermined that one day we would be like His Son. Predestination applies only to saved people. Nowhere are we taught that God predestines people to be eternally condemned. If they are condemned, it is because of their refusal to trust Christ (John 3:18–21). Those whom He chose, He called (see 2 Thess. 2:13–14); when they responded to His call, He justified them, and He also glorified them. This means that the believer has already been glorified in Christ (John 17:22); the revelation of this glory awaits the coming of the Lord (Rom. 8:21–23).

How can we Christians ever be discouraged and frustrated when we already share the glory of God? Our suffering today only guarantees that much more glory when Jesus Christ returns!

4. FREEDOM FROM FEAR—NO SEPARATION (8:31–39)

There is no condemnation because we share the righteousness of God and the law cannot condemn us. There is no obligation because we have the Spirit of God who enables us to overcome the flesh and live for God. There is no frustration because we share the glory of God, the blessed hope of Christ's return. There is no separation because we experience the love of God: "Who shall separate us from the love of Christ?" (Rom. 8:35).

The emphasis in this final section is on the security of the believer. We do not need to fear the past, present, or future because we are secure in the love of Christ. Paul presented five arguments to prove that there could be no separation between the believer and the Lord.

(1) God is for us (v. 31). *The Father* is for us and proved it by giving His Son (Rom. 8:32). *The Son* is for us (Rom. 8:34) and so is *the Spirit* (Rom. 8:26). God is making all things work for us (Rom. 8:28). In His person and His providence, God is for us. Sometimes, like Jacob, we lament, "All these

things are against me" (Gen. 42:36), when actually everything is working for us. The conclusion is obvious: "If God be for us, who can be against us?"

The believer needs to enter into each new day realizing that God is for him. There is no need to fear, for his loving Father desires only the best for His children, even if they must go through trials to receive His best. "'For I know the plans that I have for you,' declares the LORD, 'plans for welfare and not for calamity to give you a future and a hope'" (Jer. 29:11 NASB).

(2) Christ died for us (v. 32). The argument here is from the lesser to the greater. If when we were sinners, God gave us His best, now that we are God's children, will He not give us all that we need? Jesus used this same argument when He tried to convince people that it was foolish to worry and fear. God cares for the birds and sheep, and even for the lilies; surely He will care for you! God is dealing with His own on the basis of Calvary grace, not on the basis of law. God freely gives all things to His own!

(3) God has justified us (v. 33). This means that He has declared us righteous in Christ. Satan would like to accuse us (Zech. 3:1–7; Rev. 12:10), but we stand righteous in Jesus Christ. We are God's elect—chosen in Christ and accepted in Christ. God will certainly not accuse us, since it is He who has justified us. For Him to accuse us would mean that His salvation was a failure and we are still in our sins.

Understanding the meaning of justification brings peace to our hearts. When God declares the believing sinner righteous in Christ, that declaration never changes. Our Christian experience changes from day to day, but justification never changes. We may accuse ourselves, and others may accuse us, but God will never take us to court and accuse us. Jesus has already paid the penalty and we are secure in Him.

(4) Christ intercedes for us (v. 34). A dual intercession keeps the believer secure in Christ: The Spirit intercedes (Rom. 8:26–27) and the Son of God intercedes (Rom. 8:34). The same Savior who died for us is now interceding for us in heaven. As our High Priest, He can give us the grace we need to overcome temptation and defeat the enemy (Heb. 4:14–16). As our Advocate, He can forgive our sins and restore our fellowship with God (1 John 1:9—2:2). Intercession means that Jesus Christ represents us before the throne of God and we do not have to represent ourselves.

Paul hinted at this ministry of intercession in Romans 5:9–10. We are not only saved by His death, but we are also saved by His life. "Therefore he is able to save completely those who come to God through him, because he always lives to intercede for them" (Heb. 7:25 NIV). Peter sinned against the Lord, but he was forgiven and restored to fellowship because of Jesus Christ. "Simon, Simon, listen! Satan has asked permission to sift all of you like wheat, but I have prayed especially for you that your own faith may not utterly fail" (Luke 22:31–32 WMS). He is interceding for each of us, a ministry that assures us that we are secure.

(5) Christ loves us (vv. 35–39). In Romans 8:31–34 Paul proved that God cannot fail us, but is it possible that we can fail Him? Suppose some great trial or temptation comes, and we fail? Then what? Paul deals with that problem in this final section and explains that nothing can separate us from the love of Jesus Christ.

To begin with, God does not shelter us from the difficulties of life because we need them for our spiritual growth (Rom. 5:3–5). In Romans 8:28 God assures us that the difficulties of life are working *for* us and not *against* us. God permits trials to come that we might use them for our good and His glory. We endure trials for His sake (Rom. 8:36), and since we do, do you think that He will desert us? Of course not! Instead, He is closer to us when we go through the difficulties of life.

Furthermore, He gives us the power to conquer (Rom. 8:37). We are "more than conquerors," literally, "we are superconquerors" through Jesus Christ. He gives us victory and more victory! We need not fear life or death, things present or things to come, because Jesus Christ loves us and gives us the victory. This is not a promise with conditions attached: "If you do this, God will do that." This security in Christ is an established fact, and we claim it for ourselves because we are in Christ. Nothing can separate you from His love! Believe it—and rejoice in it!

A review of this wonderful chapter shows that the Christian is completely victorious. We are free from judgment because Christ died for us and we have His righteousness. We are free from defeat because Christ lives in us by His Spirit and we share His life. We are free from discouragement because Christ is coming for us and we shall share His glory. We are free from fear because Christ intercedes for us and we cannot be separated from His love.

No condemnation! No obligation! No frustration! No separation!

If God be for us, who can be against us?

QUESTIONS FOR PERSONAL REFLECTION OR GROUP DISCUSSION

1. What was Paul's message to the believers in Romans 8:1–39? How does this relate to Romans 7?

2. What is the believer's new relationship to the law?

3. What are the four spiritual freedoms summarized by Wiersbe? How do these freedoms affect your life?

4. What three statements did Paul make that add up to "no condemnation"? Do you live as if this is true?

5. What are the four contrasts mentioned concerning freedom from defeat?

6. What is the root of sin? In what area of your life do you see most evidence of this?

7. According to Romans 8:18–30, who is "groaning"? When will the groaning end?

8. What can truly give believers freedom from discouragement?

9. How can you prove that there will be no separation between the believer and the Lord?

10. How can you personally apply one or more of these freedoms to the way you view your life with God?

Chapter Eight

DID GOD
MAKE A MISTAKE?
(Romans 9)

I t seems strange that Paul would interrupt his discussion of salvation and devote a long section of three chapters to the nation of Israel. Why didn't he move from the doctrinal teaching of Romans 8 to the practical duties given in Romans 12—15? A careful study of Romans 9—11 reveals that this section is not an interruption at all; it is a necessary part of Paul's argument for justification by faith.

To begin with, Paul was considered a traitor to the Jewish nation. He ministered to Gentiles, and he taught freedom from the law of Moses. He had preached in many synagogues and caused trouble, and no doubt many of the Jewish believers in Rome had heard of his questionable reputation. In these chapters, Paul showed his love for Israel and his desire for their welfare. This is the personal reason for this discussion.

But there was a doctrinal reason. Paul argued in Romans 8 that the believer is secure in Jesus Christ and that God's election would stand (Rom. 8:28–30). But someone might ask, "What about the Jews? They were chosen by God, and yet now you tell us they are set aside and God is building His church. Did God fail to keep His promises to Israel?" In other words, the very character of God was at stake. If God was not faithful to the Jews, how do we know He will be faithful to the church?

The emphasis in Romans 9 is on Israel's past election, in Romans 10 on Israel's present rejection, and in Romans 11 on Israel's future restoration. Israel is the only nation in the world with a complete history—past, present, and future. In Romans 9, Paul defended the character of God by showing that Israel's past history actually magnified the attributes of God. He specifically named four attributes of God: His faithfulness (Rom. 9:1–13), righteousness (Rom. 9:14–18), justice (Rom. 9:19–29), and grace (Rom. 9:30–33). You will note that these divisions correspond with Paul's three questions: "Is there unrighteousness with God?" (Rom. 9:14), "Why doth he yet find fault?" (Rom. 9:19), and "What shall we say then?" (Rom. 9:30).

1. GOD'S FAITHFULNESS (9:1–13)

It is remarkable how Paul moved from the joy of Romans 8 into the sorrow and burden of Romans 9. When he looked at Christ, he rejoiced, but when he looked at the lost people of Israel, he wept. Like Moses (Ex. 32:30–35), he was willing to be cursed and separated from Christ if it would mean the salvation of Israel. What a man this Paul was! He was willing to stay out of heaven for the sake of the saved (Phil. 1:22–24), and willing to go to hell for the sake of the lost.

His theme was God's election of Israel, and the first thing he dealt with was the blessing of their election (Rom. 9:4–5). Israel was adopted by God as His own people (Ex. 4:22–23). He gave them His glory in the tabernacle and the temple (Ex. 40:34–38; 1 Kings 8:10–11). The glory Moses beheld on Mount Sinai came to dwell with Israel (Ex. 24:16–17). God gave Israel His covenants, the first to Abraham, and then additional covenants to Moses and to David. He also gave them His law to govern their political, social, and religious life, and to guarantee His blessing if they obeyed.

He gave them "the service of God," referring to the ministry in the tabernacle and the temple. He gave them the promises and the patriarchs ("the fathers" in Rom. 9:5). The purpose of all of this blessing was that Jesus Christ, through Israel, might come into the world. (Note that Rom. 9:5 affirms that Jesus Christ is God.) All of these blessings were given freely to Israel and to no other nation.

But in spite of these blessings, Israel failed. When the Messiah appeared, Israel rejected Him and crucified Him. No one knew this better than Paul, because in his early days he persecuted the church. Does Israel's failure mean that God's Word has failed? (The Greek word translated "taken none effect" pictures a ship going off its course.) The answer is, "No! God is faithful no matter what people may do with His Word." Here Paul explains the basis for Israel's election.

It was not of natural descent (vv. 6–10). As we saw in Romans 2:25–29, there is a difference between the natural seed of Abraham and the spiritual children of Abraham. Abraham actually had two sons, Ishmael (by Hagar) and Isaac (by Sarah). Since Ishmael was the firstborn, he should have been chosen, but it was Isaac that God chose. Isaac and Rebecca had twin sons, Esau and Jacob. As the firstborn, Esau should have been chosen, but it was Jacob that God chose. And Esau and Jacob had the same father and mother, unlike Ishmael and Isaac, who had the same father but different mothers. God did not base His election on the physical. Therefore, if the nation of Israel—Abraham's physical descendants—has rejected God's Word, this does not nullify God's elective purposes at all.

It is not of human merit (vv. 11–13). God chose Jacob before the babies were born. The two boys had done neither good nor evil, so God's choice was not based on their character or conduct. Romans 9:13 is a reference to Malachi 1:2–3 and refers to nations (Israel and Edom) and not individual sinners. God does not hate sinners. John 3:16 makes it clear that He loves sinners. The statement here has to do with national election, not individual. Since God's election of Israel does not depend on human merit, their disobedience cannot nullify the elective purposes of God. God is faithful even though His people are unfaithful.

2. GOD'S RIGHTEOUSNESS (9:14–18)

The fact that God chose one and not the other seems to indicate that He is unrighteous. "Is there unrighteousness with God?" Paul asked, and then he replied, "God forbid!" It is unthinkable that the holy God should ever commit an unrighteous act. Election is always totally a matter of grace. If God acted only on the basis of righteousness, nobody would ever be saved. Paul quoted Exodus 33:19 to show that God's mercy and compassion are extended according to God's will and not man's will. All of us deserve condemnation—not mercy. The reference in Exodus 33 deals with Israel's idolatry while Moses was on the mount receiving the law. The whole nation deserved to be destroyed, yet God killed only three thousand people—not because they were more wicked or less godly, but purely because of His grace and mercy.

Paul then quoted Exodus 9:16, using Pharaoh as an illustration. Moses was a Jew; Pharaoh was a Gentile, yet both were sinners. In fact, both were murderers! Both saw God's wonders. Yet Moses was saved and Pharaoh was lost. God raised up Pharaoh that He might reveal His glory and power, and He had mercy on Moses that He might use him to deliver the people of Israel. Pharaoh was a ruler, and Moses was a slave, yet it was Moses who experienced the mercy and compassion of God—because God willed it that way. God is sovereign in His work and acts according to His own will and purposes. So it was not a matter of righteousness but of the sovereign will of God.

God is holy and must punish sin, but God is loving and desires to save sinners. If everybody is saved, it would deny His holiness, but if everybody is lost, it would deny His love. The solution to the problem is God's sovereign election.

A seminary professor once said to me, "Try to explain election, and you may lose your mind; but explain it away and you will lose your soul!"

God chose Israel and condemned Egypt, because this was His sovereign purpose. Nobody can condemn God for the way He extends His mercy, because God is righteous.

Before leaving this section, we need to discuss the "hardening" of Pharaoh (Rom. 9:18). This hardening process is referred to at least fifteen times in Exodus 7—14. Sometimes we are told that Pharaoh hardened his heart (Ex. 8:15, 19, 32), and other times that God hardened Pharaoh's heart (Ex. 9:12; 10:1, 20, 27). By declaring His Word and revealing His power, God gave Pharaoh opportunity to repent, but instead, Pharaoh resisted God and hardened his heart. The fault lay not with God but Pharaoh. The same sunlight that melts the ice also hardens the clay. God was not unrighteous in His dealings with Pharaoh because He gave him many opportunities to repent and believe.

3. GOD'S JUSTICE (9:19–29)

This fact of God's sovereign will only seems to create a new problem. "If God is sovereign, then who can resist Him? And if one does resist Him, what right does He have to judge?" It is the age-old question of the justice of God as He works in human history.

I recall sharing in a street meeting in Chicago and passing out tracts at the corner of Madison and Kedzie. Most of the people graciously accepted the tracts, but one man took the tract and with a snarl crumpled it up and threw it in the gutter. The name of the tract was "Four Things God Wants You to Know."

"There are a few things I would like God to know!" the man said.

"Why is there so much sorrow and tragedy in this world? Why do the innocent suffer while the rich go free? Bah! Don't tell me there's a God! If there is, then God is the biggest sinner that ever lived!" And he turned away with a sneer and was lost in the crowd.

We know that God by nature is perfectly just. "Shall not the Judge of all the earth do right?" (Gen. 18:25). It is unthinkable that God would will an unjust purpose or perform an unjust act. But at times it seems that He does just that. He had mercy on Moses but condemned Pharaoh. Is this just? He elected Israel and rejected the other nations. Is this just? Paul gives three answers to this charge.

(1) **Who are we to argue with God (vv. 19–21)?** This is a logical argument. God is the Potter and we are the clay. God is wiser than we are, and we are foolish to question His will or to resist it. (The reference here is to Isa. 45:9.) To be sure, the clay has no life and is passive in the potter's hand. We have feelings, intellect, and willpower, and we can resist Him if we choose. (See Jer. 18, where this thought is developed.) But it is God who determines whether a man will be a Moses or a Pharaoh. Neither Moses, nor Pharaoh, nor anyone else, could choose his parents, his genetic structure, or his time and place of birth. We have to believe that these matters are in the hands of God.

However, this does not excuse us from responsibility. Pharaoh had great opportunities to learn about the true God and trust Him, and yet he chose to rebel. Paul did not develop this aspect of truth because his theme was divine sovereignty, not human responsibility. The one does not deny the other, even though our finite minds may not fully grasp them both.

(2) **God has His purposes (vv. 22–24).** We must never think that God enjoyed watching a tyrant like Pharaoh. He endured it. God said to Moses, "I have surely seen the affliction of my people ... and have heard their cry ... for I know their sorrows" (Ex. 3:7). The fact that God was

long-suffering indicates that He gave Pharaoh opportunities to be saved (see 2 Peter 3:9). The word *fitted* in Romans 9:22 does not suggest that *God* made Pharaoh a "vessel of wrath." The verb is in what the Greek grammarians call the middle voice, making it a reflexive action verb. So, it should read: *"fitted himself for* destruction." God prepares men for glory (Rom. 9:23), but sinners prepare themselves for judgment. In Moses and Israel, God revealed the riches of His mercy; in Pharaoh and Egypt, He revealed His power and wrath. Since neither deserved any mercy, God cannot be charged with injustice.

Ultimately, of course, God's purpose was to form His church from both Jews and Gentiles (Rom. 9:24). Believers today are, by God's grace, "vessels of mercy" that He is preparing for glory, a truth that reminds us of Romans 8:29–30.

(3) All of this was prophesied (vv. 25–29). First Paul quoted Hosea 2:23, a statement declaring that God would turn from the Jews and call the Gentiles. Then he cited Hosea 1:10 to prove that this new people being called would be God's people and "sons of the living God." He then quoted Isaiah 10:22–23 to show that only a remnant of Israel would be saved, while the greater part of the nation would suffer judgment. Romans 9:28 probably refers to God's work of judgment during the tribulation, when the nation of Israel will be persecuted and judged, and only a small remnant left to enter into the kingdom when Jesus Christ returns to earth. But the application for today is clear: Only a remnant of Jews is believing, and they, together with the Gentiles, are the called of God (Rom. 9:24). The final quotation from Isaiah 1:9 emphasized the grace of God in sparing the believing remnant.

Now, what does all of this prove? That God was not unjust in saving some and judging others, because He was only fulfilling the Old Testament prophecies given centuries ago. He would be unjust if He did not keep His own Word. But even more than that, these prophecies show that God's election has made possible the salvation of the Gentiles. This is the grace of God. At the Exodus, God rejected the Gentiles and chose the Jews, so that, through the Jews, He might save the Gentiles. The nation of Israel rejected His will, but this did not defeat His purposes. A remnant of Jews does believe and God's Word has been fulfilled.

So far, Paul had defended the character of God by showing His faithfulness, His righteousness, and His justice. Israel's rejection had not canceled God's election; it had only proved that He was true to His character and His purposes.

4. God's Grace (9:30–33)

Paul moved next from divine sovereignty to human responsibility. Note that Paul did not say "elect" and "nonelect," but rather emphasized faith. Here is a paradox: The Jews sought righteousness but did not find it, while the Gentiles, who were not searching for it, found it! The reason? Israel tried to be saved by works and not by faith. They rejected "grace righteousness" and tried to please God with "law righteousness." The Jews thought that the Gentiles had to *come up* to Israel's level to be saved; when actually the Jews had to *go down* to the level of the Gentiles to be saved. "For there is no difference: for all have sinned, and come short of the glory of God" (Rom. 3:22–23). Instead of permitting their religious privileges (Rom. 9:1–5) to lead them to Christ, they used these privileges as a substitute for Christ.

But see the grace of God: Israel's rejection means the Gentiles' salvation. Paul's final quotation was from Isaiah 28:16. It referred to Christ, God's Stone of salvation (see Ps. 118:22). God gave Christ to be a Foundation Stone, but Israel rejected Him and He became a stumbling stone. Instead of "rising" on this Stone, Israel fell (Rom. 11:11), but, as we shall see, their fall made possible the salvation of the Gentiles by the grace of God.

We need to decide what kind of righteousness we are seeking, whether we are depending on good works and character, or trusting Christ alone for salvation. God does not save people on the basis of birth or behavior. He saves them "by grace, through faith" (Eph. 2:8–9). It is not a question of whether or not we are among God's elect. That is a mystery known only to God. He offers us His salvation by faith. The offer is made to "whosoever will" (Rev. 22:17). After we have trusted Christ, then we have the witness and evidence that we are among His elect (Eph. 1:4–14; 1 Thess. 1:1–10). But first we must trust Him and receive by faith His righteousness that alone can guarantee heaven.

No one will deny that there are many mysteries connected with divine sovereignty and human responsibility. Nowhere does God ask us to choose between these two truths, because they both come from God and are a part of God's plan. They do not compete; they cooperate. The fact that we cannot fully understand *how* they work together does not deny the fact that they do. When a man asked Charles Spurgeon how he reconciled divine sovereignty and human responsibility, Spurgeon replied, "I never try to reconcile friends!"

But the main thrust of this chapter is clear: Israel's rejection of Christ does not deny the faithfulness of God. Romans 9 does not negate Romans 8. God is still faithful, righteous, just, and gracious, and He can be depended on to accomplish His purposes and keep His promises.

QUESTIONS FOR PERSONAL REFLECTION
OR GROUP DISCUSSION

1. Why did Paul include these chapters on the nation of Israel?

2. How do Romans 9—11 relate to the first eight chapters on justification by faith?

3. How does the theme "Be right" relate to the nation of Israel?

4. What hope is there for Israel? Why is this hope important to all of us?

5. How does Israel's past history magnify the attributes of God?

6. What is and is not the basis for salvation?

7. How can we answer the objection that it is not just for God to elect some and not others?

8. How can you reconcile divine sovereignty with human responsibility in salvation?

9. Why did the Gentiles find righteousness while most of the Jews did not?

10. How did Paul feel when he thought of his Jewish kinsmen not arriving at true righteousness? How do you feel when you think of those that are lost?

Chapter Nine

THE WRONG RIGHTEOUSNESS

(Romans 10)

T he theme of this chapter is Israel's present rejection. Paul moved from divine sovereignty (Rom. 9) to human responsibility. He continued the theme of righteousness introduced at the end of the previous chapter (Rom. 9:30–33) and explains three aspects of Israel's rejection.

1. THE REASONS FOR THEIR REJECTION (10:1–13)

You would think that Israel as a nation would have been eagerly expecting the arrival of their Messiah and been prepared to receive Him. For centuries they had known the Old Testament prophecies and had practiced the law, which was "a schoolmaster" to lead them to Christ (Gal. 3:24). God had sought to prepare the nation, but when Jesus Christ came, they rejected Him. "He came unto his own [world] and his own [people] received him not" (John 1:11). To be sure, there was a faithful remnant in the nation that looked for His arrival, such as Simeon and Anna (Luke 2:25–38), but the majority of the people were not ready when He came.

How do we explain this tragic event? Paul gives several reasons why Israel rejected their Messiah.

They did not feel a need for salvation (v. 1). There was a time when Paul would have agreed with his people, for he himself opposed the gospel and considered Jesus Christ an impostor. Israel considered the Gentiles in need of salvation, but certainly not the Jews. In several of His parables, Jesus pointed out this wrong attitude: The elder brother (Luke 15:11–32) and the Pharisee (Luke 18:9–14) are two examples. Israel would have been happy for political salvation from Rome, but she did not feel she needed spiritual salvation from her own sin.

They were zealous for God (v. 2). Ever since Israel returned to their land from Babylonian captivity, the nation had been cured of idolatry. In the temple and the local synagogues, only the true God was worshipped and served, and only the true law was taught. So zealous were the Jews that they even "improved upon God's law" and added their own traditions, making them equal to the law. Paul himself had been zealous for the law and the traditions (Acts 26:1–11; Gal. 1:13–14).

But their zeal was not based on knowledge; it was heat without light. Sad to say, many religious people today are making the same mistake. They think that their good works and religious deeds will save them, when actually these practices are keeping them from being saved. Certainly many of them are sincere and devout, but sincerity and devotion will never save the soul. "Therefore by the deeds of the law there shall no flesh be justified in his sight" (Rom. 3:20).

They were proud and self-righteous (v. 3). Israel was ignorant of God's righteousness, not because they had never been told, but because they refused to learn. There is an ignorance that comes from lack of opportunity, but Israel had had many opportunities to be saved. In their case, it was an ignorance that stemmed from willful, stubborn resistance to the truth. They would not submit to God. They were proud of their own good works and religious self-righteousness and would not admit their sins and trust the Savior. Paul had made the same mistake before he met the Lord (Phil. 3:1–11).

The godly Presbyterian preacher Robert Murray McCheyne was passing out tracts one day and handed one to a well-dressed woman. She gave him a haughty look and said, "Sir, you must not know who I am!"

In his kind way, McCheyne replied, "Madam, there is coming a day of judgment, and on that day it will not make any difference who you are."

They misunderstood their own law (vv. 4–13). Everything about the Jewish religion pointed to the coming Messiah—their sacrifices, priesthood, temple services, religious festivals, and covenants. Their law told them they were sinners in need of a Savior. But instead of letting the law bring them to Christ (Gal. 3:24), they worshipped their law and rejected their Savior. The law was a signpost, pointing the way. But it could never take them to their destination. The law cannot give righteousness; it only leads the sinner to the Savior who can give righteousness.

Christ is "the end of the law" in the sense that through His death and resurrection, He has terminated the ministry of the law for those who believe. The law is ended as far as Christians are concerned. The righteousness of the law is being fulfilled in the life of the believer through the power of the Spirit (Rom. 8:4), but the reign of the law has ended (see Eph. 2:15; Col. 2:14). "For ye are not under the law, but under grace" (Rom. 6:14).

Paul quoted from the Old Testament to prove to his readers that they did not even understand their own law. He began with Leviticus 18:5, which states the purpose of the law: If you obey it, you live.

"But we did obey it!" they would argue.

"You may have obeyed it *outwardly*," Paul would reply, "but you did not believe it from your heart." He then quoted Deuteronomy 30:12–14 and gave the passage a deeper spiritual meaning. The theme of Moses' message was "this commandment" (Deut. 30:11), referring to the Word of God. Moses argued that the Jews had no reason to disobey the Word of God because it had been clearly explained to them and it was not far from them. In fact, Moses urged them to receive the Word in their hearts (see Deut. 5:29; 6:5–12; 13:3; 30:6). The emphasis in Deuteronomy is on the heart, the inner spiritual condition, and not mere outward acts of obedience.

Paul gave us the spiritual understanding of this admonition. He saw "the commandment" or "the Word" as meaning "Christ, God's Word." So, he substituted "Christ" for "the commandment." He told us that God's way of salvation was not difficult and complicated. We do not have to go to heaven to find Christ, or into the world of the dead. He is near to us. In other words, the gospel of Christ—the Word of faith—is available and accessible. The sinner need not perform difficult works in order to be saved. All he has to do is trust Christ. The very Word on the lips of the religious Jews was the Word of faith. The very law that they read and recited pointed to Christ.

At this point Paul quoted Isaiah 28:16 to show that salvation is *by faith*: "Whosoever believeth on him shall not be ashamed." He quoted this verse before in Romans 9:33. He made it clear in Romans 10:9–10 that salvation is *by faith*—we believe in the heart, receive God's righteousness, and then confess Christ openly and without shame.

Paul's final quotation in Romans 10:13 was from Joel 2:32, to prove that this salvation is open to everyone: "For whosoever shall call upon the name of the Lord shall be saved." Paul had already proved that "there is no difference" in condemnation (Rom. 3:20–23); now he affirms that "there is no difference" in salvation. Instead of the Jew having a special righteousness of his own through the law, he was declared to be as much a sinner as the Gentile he condemned.

This entire section emphasizes the difference between law righteousness and faith righteousness. The contrasts are seen in the following summary:

Law Righteousness	*Faith Righteousness*
Only for the Jew	For "whosoever"
Based on works	Comes by faith alone
Self-righteousness	God's righteousness
Cannot save	Brings salvation
Obey the Lord	Call on the Lord
Leads to pride	Glorifies God

Having explained the reasons for Israel's rejection of God's righteousness, Paul moves into the next aspect of the subject.

2. THE REMEDY FOR THEIR REJECTION (10:14–17)

This passage is often used as the basis for the church's missionary program, and rightly so, but its first application is to the nation of Israel. The only way unbelieving Jews can be saved is by calling on the Lord. But before they can call on Him, they must believe. For the Jew, this meant believing that Jesus Christ of Nazareth truly is the Son of God and the Messiah of Israel. It also meant believing in His death and resurrection (Rom. 10:9–10). But in order to believe, they must hear the Word, for it is the Word that creates faith in the heart of the hearer (Rom. 10:17). This meant that a herald of the Word must be sent, and it is the Lord who does the sending. At this point, Paul could well have been remembering his own call to preach the Word to the Gentiles (Acts 13:1–3).

The quotation in Romans 10:15 is found in Isaiah 52:7 and Nahum 1:15. The Nahum reference had to do with the destruction of the Assyrian Empire, the hated enemies of the Jews. Nineveh was their key city, a wicked city to which God had sent Jonah some 150 years before Nahum wrote. God had patiently dealt with Nineveh, but now His judgment was going to fall. It was this "good news" that the messenger brought to the Jews, and this is what made his feet so beautiful.

Isaiah used this statement for a *future* event—the return of Christ and the establishing of His glorious kingdom. "Thy God reigneth!" (Read Isa. 52:7–10.) The messenger with the beautiful feet announced that God had defeated Israel's enemies and that Messiah was reigning from Jerusalem.

But Paul used the quotation in a *present* application: the messengers of the gospel taking the good news to Israel today. The "peace" spoken of is "peace with God" (Rom. 5:1) and the peace Christ has effected between Jews and Gentiles by forming the one body, the church (Eph. 2:13–17). The remedy for Israel's rejection is in hearing the Word of the gospel and believing on Jesus Christ.

Isaiah 53:1 was Paul's next quotation, proving that not all of Israel would obey His Word. This verse introduced one of the greatest messianic chapters in the Old Testament. Traditionally, Jewish scholars have applied Isaiah 53 to the nation of Israel rather than to Messiah, but many ancient rabbis saw in it a picture of a suffering Messiah bearing the sins of His people (see Acts 8:26–40). In Isaiah's day, the people did not believe God's Word, nor do they believe it today. John 12:37–41 cites Isaiah 53:1 to explain how the nation saw Christ's miracles and still refused to believe. Because they would not believe, judgment came on them and they could not believe.

Note that trusting Christ is not only a matter of believing, but also obeying. Not to believe in Christ is to disobey God. God "commandeth all men everywhere to repent" (Acts 17:30). Romans 6:17 also equates "believing" and "obeying." True faith must touch the will and result in a changed life.

We must never minimize the missionary outreach of the church. While this passage relates primarily to Israel, it applies to all lost souls around the world. They cannot be saved unless they call on the Lord Jesus Christ. But they cannot call unless they believe. Faith comes by hearing, so they must hear the message. How will they hear? A messenger must go to them with the message. But this means that God must call the messenger and the messenger must be sent. What a privilege it is to be one of His messengers and have beautiful feet!

As I was writing this chapter, my phone rang and one of the businessmen in our city reported another soul led to Christ. My caller had had serious spiritual problems a few years ago and I was able to help him. Since that time, he has led many to Christ, including some in his office. His phone call was to give me the good news that one of his associates had led a friend to Christ, another miracle in a spiritual chain reaction that has been going on for three years now. My friend has beautiful feet, and wherever he goes he shares the good news of the gospel.

Some of us share the news here at home, but others are sent to distant places. In spite of some closed doors, there are still more open doors for the gospel than ever before, and we have better tools to work with. My friend, the late Dr. E. Meyers Harrison, veteran missionary and professor of missions, said that there are four reasons why the church must send out missionaries: (1) *the command from above*—"go ye into all the world" (Mark 16:15); (2) *the cry from beneath*—"send him to my father's house" (Luke 16:27); (3) *the call from without*—"come over ... and help us" (Acts 16:9); and (4) *the constraint from within*—"the love of Christ constraineth us" (2 Cor. 5:14).

There remains a third aspect of Israel's rejection for Paul to discuss.

3. THE RESULTS OF THEIR REJECTION (10:18–21)

There are three results, and each of them is supported by a quotation from the Old Testament.

(1) Israel is guilty (v. 18). Someone might have argued with Paul:

"But how do you know that Israel really heard?" His reply would have been Psalm 19:4, a psalm that emphasizes the revelation of God in the world. God reveals Himself in creation (Ps. 19:1–6) and in His Word (Ps. 19:7–11). The "book of Nature" and the "book of Revelation" go together and proclaim the glory of God. Israel had the benefit of both books, for she saw God at work in nature, and she received God's written Word. Israel heard, but she would not *heed*. No wonder Jesus often had to say to the crowds, "He that hath ears to hear, let him hear" (Matt. 11:15; Mark 4:9).

(2) The message goes to the Gentiles (vv. 19–20). What marvelous grace! When Israel rejected her Messiah, God sent the gospel to the Gentiles that they might be saved. This was predicted by Moses in Deuteronomy 32:21. Paul had mentioned this truth before in Romans 9:22–26. One reason why God sent the gospel to the Gentiles was that they might provoke the Jews to jealousy (Rom. 10:19; 11:11). It was an act of grace both to the Jews and to the Gentiles. The prophet Isaiah predicted too that God would save the Gentiles (Isa. 65:1).

As you study the New Testament, you discover that "to the Jew first" is a ruling principle of operation. Jesus began His ministry with the Jews. He forbad His disciples to preach to the Gentiles or the Samaritans when He sent them on their first tour of ministry (Matt. 10:1–6). After His resurrection, He commanded them to wait in Jerusalem and to start their ministry there (Luke 24:46–49; Acts 1:8). In the first seven chapters of Acts, the ministry is to Jews and to Gentiles who were Jewish proselytes. But when the nation stoned Stephen and persecution broke loose, God sent the gospel to the Samaritans (Acts 8:1–8) and then to the Gentiles (Acts 10).

The Jewish believers were shocked when Peter went to the Gentiles (Acts 11:1–18). But he explained that it was God who sent him and that it was clear to him that Jews and Gentiles were both saved the same way—by faith in Christ. But the opposition of the legalistic Jews was so great that the churches had to call a council to discuss the issue. The record of this council is given in Acts 15. Their conclusion was that Jews and Gentiles were all saved by faith in Christ, and that a Gentile did not have to become a Jewish proselyte before he could become a Christian.

(3) God still yearns over His people (v. 21). This quotation is from Isaiah 65:2. "All day long" certainly refers to this present "day of salvation" or day of grace in which we live. While Israel as a nation has been set aside, individual Jewish people can be saved and are being saved. The phrase "all day long" makes us think of Paul's ministry to the Jews in Rome when he arrived there as a prisoner. "From morning till evening" Paul expounded the Scriptures to them and sought to convince them that Jesus is the Messiah (Acts 28:23). Through Paul, God was stretching out His arms of love to His disobedient people, yearning over them, and asking them to return. God's favor to the Gentiles did not change His love for the Jews.

God wants to use us to share the gospel with both Jews and Gentiles. God can use our feet and our arms just as He used Paul's. Jesus Christ wept over Jerusalem and longed to gather His people in His arms. Instead, those arms were stretched out on a cross where He willingly died for Jews and Gentiles alike. God is long-suffering and patient, "not willing that any should perish, but that all should come to repentance" (2 Peter 3:9). Will God's patience with Israel wear out? Is there any future for the nation? Yes, there is, as the next chapter will show.

QUESTIONS FOR PERSONAL REFLECTION
OR GROUP DISCUSSION

1. What were the reasons given in 10:1–13 for Israel's rejection of their Messiah?

2. What did Paul say was the remedy for their rejection in 10:14–17?

3. What were the results of their rejection in 10:18–21?

4. Why were the Israelites ignorant of God's righteousness?

5. How is *law righteousness* different from *faith righteousness*?

6. Where today do you see zeal without knowledge?

7. Drawing from Romans 10:14–17, what application can be made in favor of missionary work?

8. What are the four reasons Dr. Harrison finds in Scripture for the church to send out missionaries?

9. How was sending the gospel to the Gentiles an act of mercy to both the Gentiles and the Jews?

10. What does it mean to trust in Christ? How does this make you feel?

Chapter Ten

GOD IS NOT THROUGH WITH ISRAEL!

(Romans 11)

For centuries people have been puzzled by the nation of Israel. The Roman government recognized the Jewish religion, but it still called the nation *secta nefaria*—"a nefarious sect." The great historian Arnold Toynbee classified Israel as "a fossil civilization" and did not know what to do with it. For some reason, the nation did not fit into his historical theories.

Paul devoted all of Romans 11 to presenting proof that God is not through with Israel. We must not apply this chapter to the church today, because Paul is discussing a literal future for a literal nation. He called five "witnesses" to prove there was a future in God's plan for the Jews.

1. PAUL HIMSELF (11:1)

"Hath God cast away his people? God forbid! For I also am an Israelite." If God has cast away His people, then how can the conversion of the apostle Paul be explained? The fact that his conversion is presented three times in the book of Acts is significant (Acts 9; 22; 26). Certainly Dr. Luke did not write these chapters and repeat the story just to exalt Paul. No, they were written to show Paul's conversion as an illustration of the future conversion of the nation of Israel. Paul called himself "one born out of due time" (1 Cor. 15:8). In 1 Timothy 1:16 he stated that God saved him "that in me first Jesus Christ might shew forth all longsuffering, for a pattern to them which should hereafter believe on him to life everlasting."

The accounts of Paul's conversion tell very little that parallels our salvation experience today. Certainly none of us has seen Christ in glory or actually heard Him speak from heaven. We were neither blinded by the light of heaven nor thrown to the ground. In what way, then, is Paul's conversion "a pattern"? It is a picture of how the nation of Israel will be saved when Jesus Christ returns to establish His kingdom on earth. The details of Israel's future restoration and salvation are given in Zechariah 12:10—13:1. The nation shall see Him as He returns (Zech. 14:4; Acts 1:11; Rev. 1:7), recognize Him as their Messiah, repent, and receive Him. It will be an experience similar to that of Saul of Tarsus when he was on his way to Damascus to persecute Christians (Acts 9).

This is why Paul used himself as the first witness. The *fact* that he was saved does not prove that there is a future for Israel. Rather, what is important is the *way* he was saved.

2. THE PROPHET ELIJAH (11:2–10)

Israel is God's elect nation; He "foreknew" them, or chose them, and they are His. The fact that most of the nation has rejected Christ is no proof that God has finished with His people. In his day, Elijah thought that the nation had totally departed from God (see 1 Kings 19). But Elijah discovered that there was yet a remnant of true believers. He thought he was the only faithful Jew left and discovered that there were seven thousand more.

Paul referred to this "remnant" in Romans 9:27, a quotation from Isaiah 10:22–23. At no time has the entire nation of Israel been true to the Lord. God makes a distinction between Abraham's natural children and his spiritual children (Rom. 2:25–29). The fact that the Jews shared in the covenant by being circumcised did not guarantee their salvation. Like Abraham, they had to believe God in order to receive His righteousness (Rom. 4:1–5).

Note that this remnant is saved by grace and not by works (Rom. 11:5–6). Note also the parallel in Romans 9:30–33. It is impossible to mix grace and works, for the one cancels the other. Israel's main concern had always been in trying to please God with good works (Rom. 9:30—10:4). The nation refused to submit to Christ's righteousness, just as religious, self-righteous people refuse to submit today.

If a remnant had been saved, thus proving that God was not through with His people, then what had happened to the rest of the nation? They had been hardened (a better translation than "blinded" in Rom. 11:7). This was the result of their resisting the truth, just as Pharaoh's heart was hardened because he resisted the truth. Paul quoted Isaiah 29:10 to support his statement, and also referred to Deuteronomy 29:4. We would expect a pagan ruler to harden himself against the Lord, but we do not expect God's people to do so.

Romans 11:9–10 are cited from Psalm 69:22–23. This psalm is one of the most important of the messianic psalms and is referred to several times in the New Testament. (Note especially Romans 11:4, 9, 21–22.) Their "table to become a snare" means that their blessings turn into burdens and judgments. This is what happened to Israel: Their spiritual blessings should have led them to Christ, but instead they became a snare that kept them from Christ. Their very religious practices and observances became substitutes for the real experience of salvation. Sad to say, this same mistake is made today when people depend on religious rituals and practices instead of trusting in the Christ who is pictured in these activities.

Paul made it clear that the hardening of Israel is neither total nor final, and this is proof that God has a future for the nation. "[Hardness] in part is happened to Israel, until the fulness of the Gentiles be come in" (Rom. 11:25). The existence of the believing Jewish remnant today, as in Elijah's day, is evidence that God still has a plan for His people. Paul did not imitate Elijah's mistake and say, "I only am left!" He knew that there was a remnant of Israel in this world who trusted God.

3. THE GENTILES (11:11–15)

In Romans 2:1–3 Paul used the Gentiles to prove the Jews guilty of sin, but here he used the Gentiles to assure Israel of a future restoration. His logic here is beautiful. When the Jews rejected the gospel, God sent it to the Gentiles, and they believed and were saved. Three tragedies occurred in Israel: The nation *fell* (Rom. 11:11), was *lost* (Rom. 11:12, "diminished"), and was *cast away* (Rom. 11:15). None of these words suggests a *final* judgment on Israel But the amazing thing is that through Israel's fall, salvation came to the Gentiles. God promised that the Gentiles would be saved (Rom. 9:25–26), and He kept His promise. Will He not also keep His promise to the Jews?

It is important to understand that the Old Testament promises to the Gentiles were linked to Israel's "rise"—her entering into her kingdom. Prophecies like Isaiah 11 and Isaiah 60 make it clear that the Gentiles will share in Israel's kingdom. But Israel did not "rise"; *she fell!* What would God then do with the Gentiles? God introduced a new factor—the church—in which believing Jews and Gentiles are one in Christ (Eph. 2:11–22). In Ephesians 3, Paul called this new program "the mystery," meaning "the sacred secret" that was not revealed in the Old Testament. Does this mean that God has abandoned His kingdom program for Israel? Of course not! Israel is merely set aside until the time comes for God's plans for Israel to be fulfilled.

Paul stated that the Gentiles had a vital ministry to Israel. Today, the saved Gentiles provoke Israel "to jealousy" (see Rom. 10:19) because of the spiritual riches they have in Christ. Israel today is spiritually bankrupt, while Christians have "all spiritual blessings" in Christ (Eph. 1:3). (If an unsaved Jew visited the average church service, would he be provoked to *jealousy* and wish he had what we have—or would he just be provoked?)

There is a future for Israel. Paul calls it "their fulness" (Rom. 11:12) and their "receiving" (Rom. 11:15). Today, Israel is fallen spiritually, but when Christ returns, the nation will rise again. Today, Israel is cast away from God, but one day they shall be received again. God will never break His covenant with His people, and He has promised to restore them. (See Jer. 31:35–37, where God links His promises to Israel to the sun, moon, and stars.)

God will not do away with Israel — any more than he would do away with nature's law — (sun, moon etc.)

4. THE PATRIARCHS (11:16–24)

From looking at the future, Paul next looked to the past to show Israel's spiritual heritage. From the beginning, Israel was a special people, set apart by God. Paul used two illustrations to prove his argument that God was not finished with the Jews.

(1) The lump of dough (v. 16a). The reference here is to Numbers 15:17–21. The first part of the dough was to be offered up to God as a symbol that the entire lump belonged to Him. The same idea was involved in the Feast of Firstfruits, when the priest offered a sheaf to the Lord as a token that the entire harvest was His (Lev. 23:9–14). The basic idea is that when God accepts the part He sanctifies the whole.

Applying this to the history of Israel, we understand Paul's argument. God accepted the founder of the nation, Abraham, and in so doing set apart his descendants as well. God also accepted the other patriarchs, Isaac and Jacob, in spite of their sins or failings. This means that God must accept the "rest of the lump"—the nation of Israel.

(2) The olive tree (vv. 16b–24). This is a symbol of the nation of Israel (Jer. 11:16–17; Hos. 14:4–6). Please keep in mind that Paul was not discussing the relationship of individual believers to God, but the place of Israel in the plan of God. The roots of the tree support the tree; again, this was a symbol of the patriarchs who founded the nation. God made His covenants with Abraham, Isaac, and Jacob, and He cannot deny them or change them. Thus, it is God's promise to Abraham that sustains Israel even today.

Many of the Jewish people did not believe. Paul pictured them as branches broken off the tree. But he saw an amazing thing taking place: Other branches were grafted in to the tree to share in the life of the tree. These branches were the Gentiles. In Romans 11:24, Paul described this grafting in as "contrary to nature." Usually a cultivated branch is grafted into a wild tree and shares its life without producing its poor fruit. But in this case, it was the "wild branch" (the Gentiles) that was grafted into the good tree! "Salvation is of the Jews" (John 4:22).

To say that the olive tree, with its natural and grafted branches, is a picture of the church would be a great mistake. In the church, "there is no difference"; believers are "all one in Christ Jesus" (Gal. 3:28). God does not look on the members of Christ's body and see them as Jews or Gentiles. The olive tree illustrates the relationship between Jew and Gentile in the program of God. The "breaking off of the branches" is the equivalent of "the fall" (Rom. 11:11), "the diminishing" (Rom. 11:12), and "the casting away" (Rom. 11:15). To read into this illustration the matter of the eternal destiny of the individual believer is to abuse the truth Paul was seeking to communicate.

Paul warned the Gentiles that they were obligated to Israel, and therefore they dared not boast of their new spiritual position (Rom. 11:18–21). The Gentiles entered into God's plan because of faith, and not because of anything good they had done. Paul was discussing the Gentiles collectively, and not the individual experience of one believer or another.

It is worth noting that, according to Bible prophecy, the professing Gentile church will be "cut off" because of apostasy. First Timothy 4 and 2 Timothy 3, along with 2 Thessalonians 2, all indicate that the professing church in the last days will depart from the faith. *There is no hope for the apostate church, but there is hope for apostate Israel!* Why? Because of the roots of the olive tree. God will keep His promises to the patriarchs, but God will break off the Gentiles because of their unbelief.

No matter how far Israel may stray from the truth of God, the roots are still good. God is still the "God of Abraham, and the God of Isaac, and the God of Jacob" (Ex. 3:6; Matt. 22:32). He will keep His promises to these patriarchs. This means that the olive tree will flourish again!

5. GOD HIMSELF (11:25–36)

Paul saved his best witness for the last. He proved that the very character and work of God were involved in the future of Israel. People may dispute about prophecy and differ in their interpretations, but let everyone realize that he is dealing with *God's people,* Israel.

God's timing (v. 25). What has happened to Israel is all a part of God's plan, and He knows what He is doing. The hardening (or blinding, Rom. 11:7) of Israel as a nation is neither total nor final: It is partial and temporary. How long will it last? "Until the fulness of the Gentiles be come in" (Rom. 11:25). There is a "fulness" for Israel (Rom. 11:12) and for the Gentiles. Today, God in His grace is visiting the Gentiles and taking out a people for His name (Acts 15:12–14). Individual Jews are being saved, of course, but this present age is primarily a time when God is visiting the Gentiles and building His church. When this present age has run its course, and the fullness of the Gentiles has come in, then God will once more deal with the nation of Israel.

Romans 11:25 is one of several "*until* verses" in the Bible, all of which are important. (Read Matthew 23:32–39; Luke 21:24; and Psalm 110:1 for other references.) It is reassuring that God knows what time it is and that He is never late in fulfilling His will.

God's promise (v. 26). The reference here is Isaiah 59:20–21, and you ought to read Isaiah 60 to complete the picture. God has promised to save His people, and He will keep His promise. There are those who interpret this as meaning salvation to individuals through the gospel, but it is my conviction that the prophet has national conversion in mind. "All Israel shall be saved" does not mean that every Jew who has ever lived will be converted, but that the Jews living when the Redeemer returns will see Him, receive Him, and be saved. Zechariah 12—13 gives the details. It seems to me that there are too many details in these Old Testament prophecies of national restoration for Israel for us to spiritualize them and apply them to the church today.

God's covenant (vv. 27–28). This is, of course, a continuation of the quotation from Isaiah 59, but the emphasis is on the covenant of God with Israel. God chose Israel in His grace and not because of any merit in her (Deut. 7:6–11; 9:1–6). If the nation was not chosen because of its goodness, can it be rejected because of its sin? "Election" means grace, not merit. The Jewish people are "enemies" to the believing Gentiles because of their hostile attitude toward the gospel. But to God, the Jewish people are "beloved for the father's sakes." God will not break His covenant with Abraham, Isaac, and Jacob.

God's nature (v. 29). "I am the Lord, I change not" (Mal. 3:6). "God is not a man that he should lie; neither the son of man, that he should repent" (Num. 23:19). God's gifts to Israel, and God's calling of Israel, cannot be taken back or changed, or God would cease to be true to His own perfect nature. The fact that Israel may not enjoy her gifts, or live up to her privileges as an elect nation, does not affect this fact one bit. God will be consistent with Himself and true to His Word no matter what people may do. "Shall their unbelief make the faithfulness of God without effect?" (Rom. 3:3, literal translation).

God's grace (vv. 30–32). "Because of the unbelief of the Jews, you Gentiles were saved," said Paul. "Now, may it be that through your salvation Israel will come to know Christ." Note that Paul repeatedly reminded the saved Gentiles that they had a spiritual obligation to Israel to "provoke them to jealousy" (Rom. 10:19; 11:11, 14). Israel's hardness is only "in part" (Rom. 11:25), which means that individual Jews can be saved. God has included all in unbelief—Jews and Gentiles—so that *all* might have the opportunity to be saved by grace. "There is no difference." If God can save Jews by His grace and mercy today, why can He not save them in the future?

We must remember that God chose the Jews so that the Gentiles might be saved. "In thee shall all families of the earth be blessed," was God's promise to Abraham (Gen. 12:1–3). The tragedy was that Israel became exclusive and failed to share the truth with the Gentiles. They thought that the Gentiles had to become Jews in order to be saved. But God declared both Jews and Gentiles to be lost and condemned. This meant that He could have mercy on all because of the sacrifice of Christ on the cross.

God's wisdom (vv. 33–36). Having contemplated God's great plan of salvation for Jews and Gentiles, all Paul could do was sing a hymn of praise. As someone has remarked, "Theology becomes doxology." Only a God as wise as our God could take the fall of Israel and turn it into salvation for the world. His plans will not be aborted, nor will His purposes lack fulfillment. No human being can fully know the mind of the Lord, and the more we study His ways, the more we offer Him praise. Are we to conclude that God does *not* know what He is doing, and that the nation of Israel completely ruined His plans? Of course not! God is too wise to make plans that will not be fulfilled. Israel did not allow Him to rule, so He overruled.

Paul summoned five witnesses, and they all agreed: There is a future for Israel. When Israel recovers from her "fall" and enters into her "fullness," the world will experience the riches of God's grace as never before. When Jesus Christ returns and sits on David's throne to reign over His kingdom, then Israel will be "reconciled" and "received," and it will be like a resurrection.

QUESTIONS FOR PERSONAL REFLECTION
OR GROUP DISCUSSION

1. Who are the five witnesses Paul mentioned who prove there will be a future for Israel?

2. What does each witness contribute to Israel's future?

3. Why doesn't Romans 11 apply to the church today?

4. In what way is Paul's conversion "a pattern"?

5. What two illustrations did Paul use to prove that God was not finished with the Jews?

6. If believing Jews are the saved remnant, what will happen to the rest of Israel?

7. Who is included as Israel in the phrase "All Israel shall be saved"?

8. Why are Gentiles tempted to be arrogant toward the Jews? How is this still true in the world today?

9. Why is the phrase "Theology becomes doxology" often true? How can you avoid this in your own life?

10. How does Romans 11 relate to the overall theme, "Be right"?

Chapter Eleven

RIGHT RELATIONSHIPS MEAN RIGHT LIVING
(Romans 12—13)

In all of his letters, Paul concluded with a list of practical duties that were based on the doctrines he had discussed. In the Christian life, doctrine and duty always go together. What we believe helps to determine how we behave. It is not enough for us to understand Paul's doctrinal explanations. We must translate our *learning* into *living* and show by our daily lives that we trust God's Word.

The key idea in this section is *relationships.* The term "relational theology" is a relatively new one, but the idea is not new. If we have a right relationship to God, we will have a right relationship to the people who are a part of our lives. "If a man say, I love God, and hateth his brother, he is a liar" (1 John 4:20).

OUR RELATIONSHIP TO GOD (12:1–2)

This is the fourth "therefore" in the letter. Romans 3:20 is the "therefore" of condemnation, declaring that the whole world is guilty before God. Romans 5:1 is the "therefore" of justification, and Romans 8:1 the "therefore" of assurance. In Romans 12:1, we have the "therefore" of dedication, and it is this dedication that is the basis for the other relationships that Paul discussed in this section.

What is true dedication? As Paul described it here, Christian dedication involves three steps.

(1) You give God your body (v. 1). Before we trusted Christ, we used our bodies for sinful pleasures and purposes, but now that we belong to Him, we want to use our bodies for His glory. The Christian's body is God's temple (1 Cor. 6:19–20) because the Spirit of God dwells within him (Rom. 8:9). It is our privilege to glorify Christ in our bodies and magnify Christ in our bodies (Phil. 1:20–21).

Just as Jesus Christ had to take on Himself a body in order to accomplish God's will on earth, so we must yield our bodies to Christ that He might continue God's work through us. We must yield the members of the body as "instruments of righteousness" (Rom. 6:13) for the Holy Spirit to use in the doing of God's work. The Old Testament sacrifices were dead sacrifices, but we are to be living sacrifices.

There are two "living sacrifices" in the Bible, and they help us understand what this really means. The first is Isaac (Gen. 22); the second is our Lord Jesus Christ. Isaac willingly put himself on the altar and would have died in obedience to God's will, but the Lord sent a ram to take his place. Isaac "died" just the same—he died to self and willingly yielded himself to the will of God. When he got off that altar, Isaac was a living sacrifice to the glory of God.

Of course, our Lord Jesus Christ is the perfect illustration of a living sacrifice, because He actually died as a sacrifice, in obedience to His Father's will. But He arose again. And today He is in heaven as a living sacrifice, bearing in His body the wounds of Calvary. He is our High Priest (Heb. 4:14–16) and our Advocate (1 John 2:1) before the throne of God.

The verb "present" in this verse means "to present once and for all." It commands a definite commitment of the body to the Lord, just as a bride and groom in their wedding service commit themselves to each other. It is this once-for-all commitment that determines what they do with their bodies. Paul gives us two reasons for this commitment: (1) it is the right response to all that God has done for us—"I beseech you *therefore*, brethren, *by the mercies of God*" (italics mine); and (2) this commitment is our "reasonable service" or our "spiritual act of worship." This means that every day is a worship experience when your body is yielded to the Lord.

(2) You give God your mind (v. 2a). The world wants to control your mind, but God wants to transform your mind (see Eph. 4:17–24; Col. 3:1–11). This word *transform* is the same as *transfigure* in Matthew 17:2. It has come into our English language as the word *metamorphosis*. It describes a change from within. The world wants to change your mind, so it exerts pressure from without. But the Holy Spirit changes your mind by releasing power from within. If the world controls your thinking, you are a *conformer;* if God controls your thinking, you are a *transformer.*

God transforms our minds and makes us spiritually minded by using His Word. As you spend time meditating on God's Word, memorizing it, and making it a part of your inner being, God will gradually make your mind more spiritual (see 2 Cor. 3:18).

(3) You give God your will (v. 2b). Your mind controls your body, and your will controls your mind. Many people think they can control their will by willpower, but usually they fail. (This was Paul's experience as recorded in Rom. 7:15–21). It is only when we yield the will to God that His power can take over and give us the willpower (and the won't power!) that we need to be victorious Christians.

We surrender our wills to God through disciplined prayer. As we spend time in prayer, we surrender our will to God and pray, with the Lord, "Not my will, but thy will be done." We must pray about everything, and let God have His way in everything.

For many years I have tried to begin each day by surrendering my body to the Lord. Then I spend time with His Word and let Him transform my mind and prepare my thinking for that new day. Then I pray, and I yield the plans of the day to Him and let Him work as He sees best. I especially pray about those tasks that upset or worry me—and He always sees me through. To have a right relationship with God, we must start the day by yielding to Him our bodies, minds, and wills.

OUR RELATIONSHIP TO OTHER BELIEVERS (12:3–16)

Paul was writing to Christians who were members of local churches in Rome. He described their relationship to each other in terms of the members of a body. (He used this same picture in 1 Cor. 12; Eph. 4:7–16.) The basic idea is that each believer is a living part of Christ's body, and each one has a spiritual function to perform. Each believer has a gift (or gifts) to be used for the building up of the body and the perfecting of the other members of the body. In short, we belong to each other, we minister to each other, and we need each other. What are the essentials for spiritual ministry and growth in the body of Christ?

Honest evaluation (v. 3). Each Christian must know what his spiritual gifts are and what ministry (or ministries) he is to have in the local church. It is not wrong for a Christian to recognize gifts in his own life and in the lives of others. What *is* wrong is the tendency to have a false evaluation of ourselves. Nothing causes more damage in a local church than a believer who overrates himself and tries to perform a ministry that he cannot do. (Sometimes the opposite is true, and people undervalue themselves. Both attitudes are wrong.)

The gifts that we have came because of God's grace. They must be accepted and exercised by faith. We were saved "by grace, through faith" (Eph. 2:8–9), and we must live and serve "by grace through faith." Since our gifts are from God, we cannot take the credit for them. All we can do is accept them and use them to honor His name. (See 1 Cor. 15:10 for Paul's personal testimony about gifts.)

I once ministered with two men who had opposite attitudes toward their gifts: The one man constantly belittled his gifts and would not use them, and the other man constantly boasted about gifts that he did not possess. Actually, both of them were guilty of pride, because both of them refused to acknowledge God's grace and let Him have the glory. Moses made a similar mistake when God called him (Ex. 4:1–13). When the individual believers in a church know their gifts, accept them by faith, and use them for God's glory, then God can bless in a wonderful way.

Faithful cooperation (vv. 4–8). Each believer has a different gift, and God has bestowed these gifts so the local body can grow in a balanced way. But each Christian must exercise his or her gift by faith. We may not see the result of our ministry, but the Lord sees it and He blesses. Note that "exhortation" (encouragement) is just as much a spiritual ministry as preaching or teaching. Giving and showing mercy are also important gifts. To some people, God has given the ability to rule, or to administer the various functions of the church. Whatever gift we have must be dedicated to God and used for the good of the whole church.

It is tragic when any one gift is emphasized in a local church beyond all the other gifts. "Are all apostles? are all prophets? are all teachers? are all workers of miracles? Have all the gifts of healing? do all speak with tongues? do all interpret?" (1 Cor. 12:29–30). The answer to all these questions is no! And for a Christian to minimize the other gifts while he emphasizes his own gift is to deny the very purpose for which gifts are given: The benefit of the whole body of Christ. "Now to each one the manifestation of the Spirit is given for the common good" (1 Cor. 12:7 NIV).

Spiritual gifts are tools to build with, not toys to play with or weapons to fight with. In the church at Corinth, the believers were tearing down the ministry because they were abusing spiritual gifts. They were using their gifts as ends in themselves and not as a means toward the end of building up the church. They so emphasized their spiritual gifts that they lost their spiritual graces! They had the gifts of the Spirit but were lacking in the fruit of the Spirit—love, joy, peace, etc. (Gal. 5:22–23).

Loving participation (vv. 9–16). Here the emphasis is on the attitudes of those who exercise the spiritual gifts. It is possible to use a spiritual gift in an unspiritual way. Paul makes this same point in 1 Corinthians 13, the great "love chapter" of the New Testament. Love is the circulatory system of the spiritual body, which enables all the members to function in a healthy, harmonious way. This must be an honest love, not a hypocritical love (Rom. 12:9), and it must be humble, not proud (Rom. 12:10). "Preferring one another" means treating others as more important than ourselves (Phil. 2:1–4).

Serving Christ usually means satanic opposition and days of discouragement. Paul admonished his readers to maintain their spiritual zeal because they were serving the Lord and not men. When life becomes difficult, the Christian cannot permit his zeal to grow cold. "Be joyful in hope, patient in affliction, faithful in prayer" (Rom. 12:12 NIV).

Finally, Paul reminded them that they must enter into the feelings of others. Christian fellowship is much more than a pat on the back and a handshake. It means sharing the burdens and the blessings of others so that we all grow together and glorify the Lord. If Christians cannot get along with one another, how can they ever face their enemies? A humble attitude and a willingness to share are the marks of a Christian who truly ministers to the body. Our Lord ministered to the common people, and they heard Him gladly (Mark 12:37). When a local church decides it wants only a certain "high class" of people, it departs from the Christian ideal for ministry.

OUR RELATIONSHIP TO OUR ENEMIES (12:17–21)

The believer who seeks to obey God is going to have enemies. When our Lord was ministering on earth, He had enemies. No matter where Paul and the other apostles traveled, there were enemies who opposed their work. Jesus warned His disciples that their worst enemies might be those of their own household (Matt. 10:36). Unfortunately, some believers have enemies because they lack love and patience, and not because they are faithful in their witness. There is a difference between sharing in "the offense of the cross" (Gal. 5:11; 6:12–15) and being an offensive Christian!

The Christian must not play God and try to avenge himself. Returning evil for evil, or good for good, is the way most people live. But the Christian must live on a higher level and return good for evil. Of course, this requires *love*, because our first inclination is to fight back. It also requires *faith*, believing that God can work and accomplish His will in our lives and in the lives of those who hurt us. We must give place to "the wrath"—the wrath of God (Deut. 32:35).

A friend of mine once heard a preacher criticize him over the radio and say things that were not only unkind but also untrue. My friend became very angry and was planning to fight back, when a godly preacher said, "Don't do it. If you defend yourself, then the Lord can't defend you. Leave it in His hands." My friend followed that wise counsel, and the Lord vindicated him.

The admonition in Romans 12:20 reminds us of Christ's words in Matthew 5:44–48. These words are easy to read but difficult to practice. Surely we need to pray and ask God for love as we try to show kindness to our enemies. Will they take advantage of us? Will they hate us more? Only the Lord knows. Our task is not to protect ourselves but to obey the Lord and leave the results with Him. Paul referred to Proverbs 25:21–22 as he urged us to return good for evil in the name of the Lord. The "coals of fire" refer perhaps to the feeling of shame our enemies will experience when we return good for evil.

As children of God, we must live on the highest level—returning good for evil. Anyone can return good for good and evil for evil. The only way to overcome evil is with good. If we return evil for evil, we only add fuel to the fire. And even if our enemy is not converted, we have still experienced the love of God in our own hearts and have grown in grace.

OUR RELATIONSHIP TO THE STATE (13:1–14)

God has established three institutions: the home (Gen. 2:18–25), government (Gen. 9:1–17), and the church (Acts 2). Paul was writing to believers at the very heart of the Roman Empire. As yet, the great persecutions had not started but were on the way. Christianity was still considered a Jewish sect, and the Jewish religion was approved by Rome. But the day would come when it would be very difficult, if not impossible, for a Christian to be loyal to the emperor. He could not drop incense on the altar and affirm, "Caesar is god!"

In our own day, we have people who teach riot and rebellion *in the name of Christ!* They would have us believe that the Christian thing to do is to disobey the law, rebel against the authorities, and permit every person to do that which is right in his own eyes. Paul refuted this position in this chapter by explaining four reasons why the Christian must be in subjection to the laws of the state.

(1) For wrath's sake (vv. 1–4). It is God who has established the governments of the world (see Acts 17:24–28). This does not mean that He is responsible for the sins of tyrants, but only that the authority to rule comes originally from God. It was this lesson that Nebuchadnezzar had to learn the hard way. (See Dan. 4, and especially vv. 17, 25, 32.) To resist the law is to resist the God who established government in the world, and this means inviting punishment.

Rulers must bear the sword; that is, they have the power to afflict punishment and even to take life. God established human government because humankind is sinful and must have some kind of authority over us. God has given the sword to rulers, and with it the authority to punish and even to execute. Capital punishment was ordained in Genesis 9:5–6, and it has not been abolished. Even though we cannot always respect the person in office, we must respect the office, for government was ordained by God.

On more than one occasion in his ministry, Paul used the Roman law to protect his life and to extend his work. The centurions mentioned in the book of Acts appear to be men of character and high ideals. Even if government officials are not believers, they are still the "ministers of God" because He established the authority of the state.

(2) **For conscience's sake (vv. 5–7).** We move a bit higher in our motivation now. Any citizen can obey the law because of fear of punishment, but a Christian ought to obey because of conscience. Of course, if the government interferes with conscience, then the Christian must obey God rather than men (Acts 5:29). But when the law is right, the Christian must obey it if he is to maintain a good conscience (1 Tim. 1:5, 19; 3:9; 4:2; Acts 24:16).

The United States Government maintains a "Conscience Fund" for people who want to pay their debts to the government and yet remain anonymous. Some city governments have a similar fund. I read about a city that had investigated some tax frauds and announced that several citizens were going to be indicted. They did not release the names of the culprits. That week, a number of people visited the City Hall to "straighten out their taxes"—and many of them were not on the indictment list. When conscience begins to work, we cannot live with ourselves until we have made things right.

Romans 13:7 commands us to pay what we owe: taxes, revenue, respect, honor. If we do not pay our taxes, we show disrespect to the law, the officials, and the Lord. And this cannot but affect the conscience of the believer. We may not agree with all that is done with the money we pay in taxes, but we dare not violate our conscience by refusing to pay.

(3) For love's sake (vv. 8–10). Paul enlarged the circle of responsibility by including other people besides government officials. "Love one another" is the basic principle of the Christian life. It is the "new commandment" that Christ gave to us (John 13:34). When we practice love, there is no need for any other laws, because love covers it all. If we love others, we will not sin against them. This explained why the Ten Commandments were not referred to often in the New Testament. In fact, the Sabbath commandment is not quoted at all in any of the Epistles. As believers, we do not live under the law; we live under grace. Our motive for obeying God and helping others is the love of Christ in our hearts.

Does "owe no man anything" refer also to the Christian's financial practices? Some people believe that it does, and that it is a sin to have a debt. J. Hudson Taylor, the godly missionary to China, would never incur a debt, basing his conviction on this verse. Charles Spurgeon, the great Baptist preacher, had the same conviction. However, the Bible does not forbid borrowing or legal financial transactions that involve interest. What the Bible does forbid is the charging of high interest, robbing the brethren, and failing to pay honest debts (see Ex. 22:25–27; Neh. 5:1–11). Matthew 25:27 and Luke 19:23 indicate that banking and investing for gain are not wrong. Certainly no one should get into unnecessary debt or sign contracts he cannot maintain. "Thou shalt not steal." But to make Romans 13:8 apply to all kinds of legal obligations involving money is, to me, stretching a point.

In this section, Paul has centered on the very heart of the problem—the human heart. Because the heart of humankind is sinful, God established government. But laws cannot change the heart; humankind's heart is still selfish and can be changed only by the grace of God.

(4) For Jesus' sake (vv. 11–14). We have come a long way in our reasons for obeying the law: from fear to conscience to love to our devotion to Jesus Christ. The emphasis is on the imminent return of Christ. As His servants, we want to be found faithful when He returns. The completion of our salvation is near! The light is dawning! Therefore, be ready!

Paul gave several admonitions in the light of the Lord's soon return. The first is, "Wake up!" Relate this with 1 Thessalonians 5:1–11, and also Matthew 25:1–13. The second is, "Clean up!" We do not want to be found dressed in dirty garments when the Lord returns (1 John 2:28—3:3). The Christian wears the armor of light, not the deeds of darkness. He has no reason to get involved in the sinful pleasures of the world. Finally, Paul admonished, "Grow up" (Rom. 13:14). To "put on" the Lord Jesus Christ means to become more like Him, to receive by faith all that He is for our daily living. We grow on the basis of the food we eat. This is why God warns us not to make provisions for the flesh. If we feed the flesh, we will fail, but if we feed the inner being the nourishing things of the Spirit, we will succeed.

In other words, a Christian citizen ought to be the best citizen. Christians may not always agree on politics or parties, but they can all agree on their attitude toward human government.

QUESTIONS FOR PERSONAL REFLECTION
OR GROUP DISCUSSION

1. What are the connections between these pairs: doctrine and duty, beliefs and behavior, learning and living? How are these related to relationships?

2. What are the three steps in Christian dedication that Paul gave in Romans 12:1–2?

3. How does God transform our minds? What is our part in this?

4. How can we surrender our wills to the Lord?

5. What does Wiersbe believe are the essentials for spiritual ministry and growth in the body of Christ?

6. In what two extreme ways can a believer act inappropriately with regard to his or her spiritual gifts?

7. What are two marks of a Christian who is ministering effectively in the body? How can you better see these marks in your own life?

8. When wrongs are done to us, what is the proper response? Why is this so difficult? When have you battled with loving your enemies?

9. Why must the Christian be subject to the laws of the government? Are there any exceptions?

10. What does it mean to "put on" the Lord Jesus Christ?

Chapter Twelve

WHEN CHRISTIANS DISAGREE

(Romans 14:1—15:7)

Disunity has always been a major problem with God's people. Even the Old Testament records the civil wars and family fights among the people of Israel, and almost every local church mentioned in the New Testament had divisions to contend with. The Corinthians were divided over human leaders, and some of the members were even suing each other (1 Cor. 1:10–13; 6:1–8). The Galatian saints were "biting and devouring" one another (see Gal. 5:15), and the saints in Ephesus and Colossae had to be reminded of the importance of Christian unity (Eph. 4:1–3; Col. 2:1–2). In the church at Philippi, two women were at odds with each other and, as a result, were splitting the church (Phil. 4:1–3). No wonder the psalmist wrote, "Behold, how good and how pleasant it is for brethren to dwell together in unity" (Ps. 133:1).

Some of these problems stemmed from the backgrounds of the believers in the churches. The Jews, for example, were saved out of a strict legalistic background that would be difficult to forget. The Gentiles never had to worry about diets and days. The first church council in history debated the issue of the relationship of the Christian to the law (Acts 15).

The believers in Rome were divided over special diets and special days.

Some of the members thought it was a sin to eat meat, so they ate only vegetables. Other members thought it a sin not to observe the Jewish holy days. If each Christian had kept his convictions to himself, there would have been no problem, but they began to criticize and judge one another. The one group was sure the other group was not at all spiritual.

Unfortunately, we have similar problems today with many gray areas of life that are not clearly right or wrong to every believer. Some activities we know are wrong, because the Bible clearly condemns them. Other activities we know are right, because the Bible clearly commands them. But when it comes to areas that are not clearly defined in Scripture, we find ourselves needing some other kind of guidance. Paul gave principles of this guidance. He explained how believers could disagree on nonessentials and still maintain unity in the church. He gave his readers three important admonitions.

1. Receive One Another (14:1–12)

You will note that this section begins and ends with this admonition (Rom. 15:7). Paul was addressing those who were strong in the faith, that is, those who understood their spiritual liberty in Christ and were not enslaved to diets or holy days. The "weak in faith" were immature believers who felt obligated to obey legalistic rules concerning what they ate and when they worshipped. Many people have the idea that the Christians who follow strict rules are the most mature, but this is not necessarily the case. In the Roman assemblies, the weak Christians were those who clung to the law and did not enjoy their freedom in the Lord. The weak Christians were judging and condemning the strong Christians, and the strong Christians were despising the weak Christians.

"Welcome one another!" was Paul's first admonition, and he gave four reasons why they should.

(1) God has received us (vv. 1–3). It is not our responsibility to decide the requirements for Christian fellowship in a church; only the Lord can do this. To set up man-made restrictions on the basis of personal prejudices (or even convictions) is to go beyond the Word of God. Because God has received us, we must receive one another. We must not argue over these matters, nor must we judge or despise one another. Perhaps St. Augustine put the matter best: "In essentials, unity; in nonessentials, liberty; in all things, charity."

When God sent Peter to take the gospel to the Gentiles, the church criticized Peter because he ate with these new Christians (Acts 11:1–3). But God had clearly revealed His acceptance of the Gentiles by giving them the same Holy Spirit that He bestowed on the Jewish believers at Pentecost (Acts 10:44–48; 11:15–18). Peter did not obey this truth consistently, for later on he refused to fellowship with the Gentile Christians in Antioch, and Paul had to rebuke him (Gal. 2:11–13). God showed both Peter and Paul that Christian fellowship was not to be based on food or religious calendars.

In every church there are weak and strong believers. The strong understand spiritual truth and practice it, but the weak have not yet grown into that level of maturity and liberty. The weak must not condemn the strong and call them unspiritual. The strong must not despise the weak and call them immature. God has received both the weak and the strong; therefore, they should receive one another.

(2) God sustains His own (v. 4). The strong Christian was judged by the weak Christian, and this Paul condemned because it was wrong for the weak Christian to take the place of God in the life of the strong Christian. God is the Master; the Christian is the servant. It is wrong for anyone to interfere with this relationship.

It is encouraging to know that our success in the Christian life does not depend on the opinions or attitudes of other Christians. God is the

Judge, and He is able to make us stand. The word *servant* here suggests that Christians ought to be busy working for the Lord; then they will not have the time or inclination to judge or condemn other Christians. People who are busy winning souls to Christ have more important things to do than to investigate the lives of the saints!

(3) Jesus Christ is Lord (vv. 5–9). The word *Lord* is found eight times in these verses. No Christian has the right to "play God" in another Christian's life. We can pray, advise, and even admonish, but we cannot take the place of God. What is it that makes a dish of food "holy" or a day "holy"? It is the fact that we relate it to the Lord. The person who treats a special day as "holy" does so "unto the Lord." The person who treats every day as sacred, does so "unto the Lord." The Christian who eats meat gives thanks to the Lord, and the Christian who abstains from meat abstains "unto the Lord." To be "fully persuaded [or assured] in his own mind" (Rom. 14:5) means "Let every man see to it that he is really doing what he does for the Lord sake, and not merely on the basis of some prejudice or whim."

Some standards and practices in our local churches are traditional but not necessarily scriptural. Some of us can remember when dedicated Christians opposed Christian radio "because Satan was the prince of the power of the air!" Some people even make Bible translations a test of orthodoxy. The church is divided and weakened because Christians will not allow Jesus Christ to be Lord.

An interesting illustration of this truth is given in John 21:15–25. Jesus had restored Peter to his place as an apostle, and once again He told him, "Follow me." Peter began to follow Christ, but then he heard someone walking behind him. It was the apostle John.

Then Peter asked Jesus, "Lord ... what shall this man do?"

Notice the Lord's reply: "What is that to thee? Follow thou me!" In other words, "Peter, you make sure you have made Me Lord of your life. Let

Me worry about John." Whenever I hear believers condemning other Christians because of something they disagree with, something that is not essential or forbidden in the Word, I feel like saying, "What is that to thee? Follow Christ! Let Him be the Lord!"

Paul emphasized the believer's union with Christ: "Whether we live, therefore, or die, we are the Lord's" (see Rom. 14:8). Our first responsibility is to the Lord. If Christians would go to the Lord in prayer instead of going to their brother with criticism, there would be stronger fellowship in our churches.

(4) Jesus Christ is Judge (vv. 10–12). Paul asked the weak Christian, "Why are you judging your brother?" Then he asked the strong Christian, "Why are you despising your brother?" Both strong and weak must stand at the judgment seat of Christ, and they will not judge each other—they will be judged by the Lord.

The judgment seat of Christ is that place where Christians will have their works judged by the Lord. It has nothing to do with our sins, since Christ has paid for them and they can be held against us no more (Rom. 8:1). The word for "judgment seat" in the Greek is *bema,* meaning the place where the judges stood at the athletic games. If during the games they saw an athlete break the rules, they immediately disqualified him. At the end of the contests, the judges gave out the rewards (see 1 Cor. 9:24–27). First Corinthians 3:10–15 gives another picture of the judgment seat of Christ. Paul compared our ministries with the building of a temple. If we build with cheap materials, the fire will burn them up. If we use precious, lasting materials, our works will last. If our works pass the test, we receive a reward. If they are burned up, we lose the reward, but we are still saved "yet so as by fire."

How does the Christian prepare for the judgment seat of Christ? By making Jesus Lord of his life and faithfully obeying Him. Instead of judging other Christians, we had better judge our own lives and make sure we are ready to meet Christ at the *bema* (see Luke 12:41–48; Heb. 13:17; 1 John 2:28).

The fact that our sins will never be brought up against us should not encourage us to disobey God. Sin in our lives keeps us from serving Christ as we should, and this means loss of reward. Lot is a good example of this truth (Gen. 18—19). Lot was not walking with the Lord as was his uncle, Abraham, and as a result, he lost his testimony even with his own family. When the judgment finally came, Lot was spared the fire and brimstone, but everything he lived for was burned up. He was saved "yet so as by fire."

Paul explained that they did not have to give an account for anyone else but themselves. So they were to make sure that their account would be a good one. He was stressing the principle of lordship—make Jesus Christ the Lord of your life, and let Him be the Lord in the lives of other Christians as well.

Two of the most famous Christians in the Victorian Era in England were Charles Spurgeon and Joseph Parker, both of them mighty preachers of the gospel. Early in their ministries they fellowshipped and even exchanged pulpits. Then they had a disagreement, and the reports even got into the newspapers. Spurgeon accused Parker of being unspiritual because he attended the theater. Interestingly enough, Spurgeon smoked cigars, a practice many believers would condemn. Who was right? Who was wrong? Perhaps *both* of them were wrong! When it comes to questionable matters in the Christian life, cannot dedicated believers disagree without being disagreeable? "I have learned that God blesses people I disagree with!" a friend of mine told me one day, and I have learned the same thing. When Jesus Christ is Lord, we permit Him to deal with His own servants as He wishes.

2. EDIFY ONE ANOTHER (14:13–23)

If we stopped with the first admonition, it might give the impression that Christians were to leave each other alone and let the weak remain weak. But this second admonition explains things further. The emphasis is not on "master-servant" but on "brother." It is the principle of brotherly love. If we love each other, we will seek to edify each other, build each other up in the faith. Paul shared several facts to help his readers help their brethren.

Christians affect each other (vv. 13–15). Note the possible ways we can affect each other. We can cause others to stumble, grieve others, or even destroy others. Paul was speaking of the way the strong Christian affected the weak Christian. Paul dealt with a similar problem in 1 Corinthians 8—9, where the question was, "Should Christians eat meat that has been offered to idols in heathen temples?" There he pointed out that knowledge and love must work together. "Knowledge puffs up, but love builds up" (1 Cor. 8:1 NIV). The strong Christian has spiritual knowledge, but if he does not practice love, his knowledge will hurt the weak Christian. Knowledge must be balanced by love.

Often little children are afraid of the dark and think there is something hiding in the closet. Of course, Mother knows that the child is safe, but her knowledge alone cannot assure or comfort the child. You can never argue a child into losing fear. When the mother sits at the bedside, talks lovingly to the child, and assures him that everything is secure, then the child can go to sleep without fear. Knowledge plus love helps the weak person grow strong.

"There is nothing unclean of itself," Paul wrote (Rom. 14:14). No foods are unclean, no days are unclean, no people are unclean. (Read Acts 10 to see how Peter learned this lesson.) What something *does* to a person determines its quality. One man may be able to read certain books and not be bothered by them, while a weaker Christian reading the same books might be tempted to sin. But the issue is not "How does it affect me?" so much as "If I do this, how will it affect my brother?" Will it make him stumble? Will it grieve him or even destroy him by encouraging him to sin? Is it really worth it to harm a brother just so I can enjoy some food? No!

Christians must have priorities (vv. 16–18). Like the Pharisees of old, we Christians have a way of majoring on the minor things (Matt. 23:23–24). I have seen churches divided over matters that were really insignificant when compared with the vital things of the Christian faith. I have heard of churches being split over such minor matters as the location of the piano in the auditorium and the serving of meals on Sundays. "The kingdom of God is not meat and drink" (Rom. 14:17). "Food does not bring us near to God; we are no worse if we do not eat, and no better if we do" (1 Cor. 8:8 NIV).

Not the externals but the eternals must be first in our lives: righteousness, peace, and joy. Where do they come from? The Holy Spirit of God at work in our lives (see Rom. 5:1–4). If each believer would yield to the Spirit and major in a godly life, we would not have Christians fighting with each other over minor matters. Spiritual priorities are essential to harmony in the church.

Christians must help each other grow (vv. 19–21). Both the strong believer and the weak believer need to grow. The strong believer needs to grow in *love;* the weak believer needs to grow in *knowledge.* So long as a brother is weak in the faith, we must lovingly deal with him in his immaturity. But if we really love him, we will help him to grow. It is wrong for a Christian to remain immature, having a weak conscience.

An illustration from the home might help us better understand what is involved. When a child comes into a home, everything has to change. Mother and Father are careful not to leave the scissors on the chair or anything dangerous within reach. But as the child matures, it is possible for the parents to adjust the rules of the house and deal with him in a more adult fashion. It is natural for a child to stumble when he is learning to walk. But if an adult constantly stumbles, we know something is wrong.

Young Christians need the kind of fellowship that will protect them and encourage them to grow. But we cannot treat them like babies all their lives! The older Christians must exercise love and patience and be careful not to cause them to stumble. But the younger Christians must "grow in grace and in the knowledge of our Lord and Saviour Jesus Christ" (2 Peter 3:18). As they mature in the faith, they can help other believers to grow. To gear the ministry of a Sunday school class or local church only to the baby Christians is to hinder their growth as well as the ministry of the more mature saints. The weak must learn from the strong, and the strong must love the weak. The result will be peace and maturity to the glory of God.

Christians must not force their opinions on others (vv. 22–23). There are certain truths that all Christians must accept because they are the foundation for the faith. But areas of honest disagreement must not be made a test of fellowship. If you have a sincere conviction from God about a matter, keep it to yourself and do not try to force everybody else to accept it. No Christian can "borrow" another Christian's convictions and be honest in his Christian life. Unless he can hold them and practice them "by faith," he is sinning. Even if a person's convictions are immature, he must never violate his conscience. This would do great damage to his spiritual life. For example, the mature Christian knows that an idol is nothing. But a young Christian, just converted out of pagan idolatry, would still have fears about idols. If the strong believer forced the new Christian to eat meat sacrificed to an idol, the younger Christian would experience problems in his conscience that would only further weaken it (see 1 Cor. 8—9).

Conscience is strengthened by knowledge. But knowledge must be balanced by love; otherwise it tears down instead of building up. The truth that all foods are clean (Rom. 14:14, 20) will not of itself make a Christian grow. When this truth is taught in an atmosphere of love, then the younger Christian can grow and develop a strong conscience. Believers may hold different convictions about many matters, but they must hold them in love.

3. PLEASE ONE ANOTHER (15:1–7)

Paul classified himself with the strong saints as he dealt with a basic problem—*selfishness*. True Christian love is not selfish; rather, it seeks to share with others and make others happy. It is even willing to carry the younger Christians, to help them along in their spiritual development. We do not endure them. We encourage them!

Of course, the great example in this is our Lord Jesus Christ. He paid a tremendous price in order to minister to us. Paul quoted Psalm 69:9 to prove his point. Does a strong Christian think he is making a great sacrifice by giving up some food or drink? Then let him measure his sacrifice by the sacrifice of Christ. No sacrifice we could ever make could match Calvary.

A person's spiritual maturity is revealed by his discernment. He is willing to give up his rights that others might be helped. He does this, not as a burden, but as a blessing. Just as loving parents make sacrifices for their children, so the mature believer sacrifices to help younger Christians grow in the faith.

Paul shared the two sources of spiritual power from which we must draw if we are to live to please others: the Word of God (Rom. 15:4) and prayer (Rom. 15:5–6). We must confess that we sometimes get impatient with younger Christians, just as parents become impatient with their children. But the Word of God can give us the patience and encouragement that we need. Paul closed this section praying for his readers, that they might experience from God that spiritual unity that He alone can give.

This suggests to us that the local church must major in the Word of God and prayer. The first real danger to the unity of the church came because the apostles were too busy to minister God's Word and pray (Acts 6:1–7). When they found others to share their burdens, they returned to their proper ministry, and the church experienced harmony and growth.

The result of this is, of course, glory to God (Rom. 15:7). Disunity and disagreement do not glorify God; they rob Him of glory. Abraham's words to Lot are applicable to today: "Let there be no strife, I pray thee, between me and thee ... for we be brethren" (Gen. 13:8). The neighbors were watching! Abraham wanted them to see that he and Lot were different from them because they worshipped the true God. In His prayer in John 17, Jesus prayed for the unity of the church to the glory of God (John 17:20–26). Receive one another; edify one another; and please one another—all to the glory of God.

QUESTIONS FOR PERSONAL REFLECTION
OR GROUP DISCUSSION

1. What principles of guidance did Paul give for gray areas? What are some examples of these areas? Which do you struggle with?

2. Why do believers sometimes disagree over what is considered "gray"?

3. Who are described as weak Christians and who are described as strong Christians? Why is this? Where would you put yourself in this spectrum?

4. What does Romans 14:1–12 say about receiving one another? How would you rate yourself in this area?

5. How can we edify one another according to Romans 14:13–23?

6. What can we do to please one another in view of Romans 15:1–7?

7. What does it mean to have Jesus as Lord? How does that affect our judgment of other believers?

8. In order to put aside selfishness and please others, we must draw on what two sources of spiritual power? How much of a priority have you made this?

9. What does it mean for believers to be "likeminded one toward another" (15:5)?

10. How do these ideas apply in our local church? Where is your church doing well? Where could it improve?

Chapter Thirteen

MAN ON THE MOVE

(Romans 15:8—16:27)

One of the key words in the closing chapters of Romans is *ministry*. In fact, Paul uses three different Greek words to discuss the theme. In Romans 15:8, 25, 31; and 16:1, he uses the simple word for a servant or service. Our English word *deacon* comes from this word. In Romans 15:16 and 27 (the word *minister*), he used the ordinary word for service in public office or in the temple. In Romans 15:16 he used a word that is found nowhere else in the Greek New Testament, and it means "to perform sacred rites, to minister in a priestly service."

In this section, Paul explained four different ministries.

1. THE MINISTRY OF JESUS CHRIST TO THE GENTILES (15:8–13)

The supreme example of ministry must always be Jesus Christ. "But I am among you as he that serveth" (Luke 22:27). He came first of all to minister to the Jews, that through Israel He might be able to minister to the Gentiles. "To the Jew first" is a principle that was followed in the earthly ministry of Christ and in the early ministry of the church.

For example, John the Baptist came to minister to the nation of Israel to prepare them for their Messiah. When Jesus began His ministry, it was only to the people of Israel. When He sent out the apostles on their first evangelistic mission, He ordered them, "Go not into the way of the Gentiles, and into any city of the Samaritans enter ye not; but go rather to the lost sheep of the house of Israel" (Matt. 10:5–6). This does not mean that He ignored individual Gentiles, because He did minister to a few (Matt. 8:5–13; 15:21–28), but His major emphasis was on Israel.

After His resurrection, He commanded the apostles to remain in Jerusalem and begin their ministry there (Luke 24:44–49). The period covered by Acts 1—7 is characterized by a ministry only to Jews or Jewish proselytes. It was not until Acts 8 that the gospel went to the Samaritans; in Acts 10 it went to the Gentiles. Then, through the ministry of Paul, it went throughout the Roman Empire (Acts 13:1–3).

When He came and died, Jesus Christ confirmed the promises that God made to Abraham and the other "fathers" of the Jewish nation (see Luke 1:30–33, 46–55, 67–80). Some of these promises have already been fulfilled, but many await fulfillment when He returns to earth to establish His kingdom.

Was it selfish of God to emphasize the Jews? No, because through the Jews, He would send the good news of salvation to the Gentiles. The first Christians were Jewish believers. "Salvation is of the Jews" (John 4:22). In the Old Testament period, God chose Israel to be a minister to the Gentiles, but instead, Israel copied the idolatrous ways of the Gentiles and had to be chastened. In the New Testament period, God chose Jewish believers to carry the good news to the Gentiles, and they obeyed Him.

There is a beautiful progression in the promises that Paul quoted in Romans 15:9–12.

1. The Jews glorify God *among* the Gentiles (Rom. 15:9, quoting Ps. 18:49).

2. The Gentiles rejoice *with* the Jews (Rom. 15:10, quoting Deut. 32:43).

3. All the Jews and Gentiles *together* praise God (Rom. 15:11, quoting Ps. 117:1).

4. Christ shall reign over Jews and Gentiles (Rom. 15:12, quoting Isa. 11:10).

Romans 15:8 covers the period of the gospels and Acts 1—7. Romans 15:9 describes the ministry of Paul as he witnessed among the Gentiles. Romans 15:10 could be applied to the church council in Acts 15 when the Gentiles were given equal status "with his people." Today, Jews and Gentiles in the church are praising God together.

The word *trust* at the end of Romans 15:12 is actually the word for *hope*. At one time the Gentiles were "without hope" (Eph. 2:12 NIV), but now in Christ they have hope. Not only do believers have hope, but they also have joy and peace and power (Rom. 15:13). The Holy Spirit of God shares these blessings with them as they yield to Him.

Because the Jewish Christians were faithful to take the gospel to the Gentiles, the nations of the world today have the opportunity to trust Christ as Savior.

2. Paul's Ministry to the Gentiles (15:14–24)

Unless we understand the distinctive ministry of Paul, we will not fully appreciate the message of God's grace. Paul explained the characteristics of his ministry.

It was received by grace (vv. 14–15). When he was Saul of Tarsus, Paul knew little of the grace of God. He persecuted the church and sought to destroy it. When Paul met Jesus Christ on the Damascus road (Acts 9), he experienced the grace of God. It was God's grace that saved him, and it was God's grace that called him and made him an apostle (1 Cor. 15:8–11). "We have received grace and apostleship, for obedience to the faith among all nations, for his name" (Rom. 1:5). In Ephesians 3, Paul explained his ministry to the Gentiles in greater detail.

It was centered in the gospel (v. 16). As mentioned before, Paul used two different words for *minister* in this verse, but the emphasis is on priestly service. Paul looked on himself as a priest at the altar, offering up to God the Gentiles he had won to Christ. They were a "spiritual sacrifice" to the glory of God (see 1 Peter 2:5). Even his preaching of the gospel was a "priestly duty" (NIV). This insight into ministry certainly adds dignity and responsibility to our service. It was important that the priests offer to God only that which was the best (see Mal. 1:6–14).

Note the involvement of the Trinity in the ministry of the Word. Paul was the minister of Jesus Christ; he preached "the gospel of God"; and he served in the power of the Holy Spirit of God who sanctified his ministry. What a privilege, and yet what a responsibility, to be the servant of the Triune God, winning the lost to Jesus Christ! We must remember that soul winning is a priestly ministry, a sacred obligation. And we must serve the Lord with dedication and devotion just as the priest served in the temple.

It was done for God's glory (v. 17). "Therefore I glory in Christ Jesus in my service to God" (NIV). The word translated "glory" carries the idea of "boast, take pride in." Paul used it before in Romans 2:17, 23; 3:27; 4:2; and 5:2–3, 11 ("joy"). Paul was not bragging about his ministry. He was boasting in what the Lord had done. The apostle did not serve and suffer as he did just to make a name for himself, for he had a much higher purpose in mind. He wanted to bring glory to Jesus Christ, "that in all things he might have the preeminence" (Col. 1:18).

It was done by God's power (vv. 18–19). The Holy Spirit empowered Paul to minister, and enabled him to perform mighty signs and wonders. The miracles God gave Paul to do were "signs" in that they came from God and revealed Him to others. And they were "wonders" in that they aroused the wonder of the people. But their purpose was always to open the way for the preaching of the gospel. Miracles were given to authenticate the messenger and the message (Heb. 2:1–4). Miracles *by themselves* can never save the lost. When Paul healed the crippled man at Lystra (Acts 14), the immediate response was pagan: The people called Paul and Barnabas gods and tried to worship them! When Paul shared the gospel with them, they did not respond so enthusiastically. Finally, the people stoned Paul and left him for dead outside the city walls.

The Spirit of God empowered Paul to share the Word, and the purpose was "to make the Gentiles obedient" (Rom. 15:18). It was "by word and deed" that the apostle shared the good news.

We may not be able to perform miracles today, since this was a special apostolic gift. But "by word and deed" we can share the love of God with the lost around us. Changes in conduct and character are just as much miracles as the healing of the sick.

It was according to God's plan (vv. 20–24). God had a special plan for Paul to follow: He was not to preach where any other apostle had ministered. (This is one evidence that Peter had not founded the churches at Rome, or had been to Rome, for this would have prevented Paul from going there.) "From Jerusalem, and round about unto Illyricum" (Rom. 15:19) covers about fourteen thousand miles! When you consider the slowness of travel and the dangers involved (2 Cor. 11:26–27), you can appreciate the tremendous achievement of Paul's missionary ministry. While it is not wrong to enter into another person's labors (John 4:38), it is also good to have a pioneer ministry and take the gospel to new territory. Paul cited Isaiah 52:15 as the divine approval for this kind of ministry.

The vast area of opportunity in other parts of the empire kept Paul from visiting Rome sooner. He was not hindered from going to Rome by satanic opposition or physical obstacles, but by the challenge of completing his work right where he was. He was so faithful in his evangelistic outreach that he was able to say that he had no more places to minister in those parts. This did not mean that Paul personally witnessed to every person in that area, but that he took the gospel and left behind witnessing churches and Christians who would carry on the work. Paul finished one job before he started another one, a good example for our evangelistic ministry today.

Paul's desire for many years had been to visit Rome and then move on to Spain, but there is no record that he ever did so. Tradition says that he did go to Spain, and possibly to Britain, after he was released, but church tradition is not always to be trusted.

3. The Gentiles' Ministry to the Jews (15:25–33)

Paul and his associates had received a special offering from the Gentile churches in Greece for the suffering Jewish saints in Jerusalem. Details about this collection are recorded in 2 Corinthians 8—9. There were several purposes behind this special offering. To begin with, it was an expression of love on the part of the Gentiles toward their Jewish brethren. Second, it meant practical relief at a time when the poor Jewish believers needed it the most. Third, it helped to unite Jews and Gentiles in the church. It was a bond that brought them closer together.

Paul looked on this offering as the paying of a debt. The Gentiles had received *spiritual* wealth from the Jews. They now returned *material* wealth, paying their debt. Paul considered himself a "debtor" to the whole world (Rom. 1:14). He also considered the Gentile Christians debtors to the Jews, for it was the Jews who gave to the Gentiles the Word of God and the Son of God. We Christians ought to feel an obligation to Israel, and to pay that debt by praying for Israel, sharing the gospel, and helping in a material way. Anti-Semitism has no place in the life of a dedicated Christian.

Not only was this offering a payment of a debt, but it was also "fruit" (Rom. 15:28). It was not "loot" that Paul stole from the churches! It was fruit—the natural result of their walk with the Lord (see John 15:1–8).

When the life of the Spirit flows through a church, giving is no problem. Paul, in 2 Corinthians 8:1–5, described the miracle of grace that occurred in the churches of Macedonia.

Paul was anxious that this offering be received by the Jewish believers and be acceptable to them. He wanted to bring about, under God, a closer bond between the mother church at Jerusalem and the daughter churches in other parts of the empire. Unfortunately, there were still Jews who opposed the message of grace to the Gentiles and who wanted the Gentiles to become Jews and accept the Jewish law. (Bible students call these people "Judaizers." They followed Paul wherever he went and tried to steal his churches from him. The epistle to the Galatians was written to combat their evil works.)

The words "strive together" in Romans 15:30 suggest an athlete giving his best in the contest. Perhaps the words "wrestling together" better express the idea. This same term is used of the praying of Epaphras in Colossians 4:12. This verse does not mean that we must fight with God to get what we need. Rather, it means our praying must not be a casual experience that has no heart or earnestness. We should put as much fervor into our praying as a wrestler does into his wrestling!

4. THE BELIEVERS' MINISTRY TO PAUL (16:1–27)

What a remarkable chapter! In it Paul greeted at least twenty-six people by name, as well as two unnamed saints, and he also greeted several churches that were meeting in homes. He closed with greetings from nine believers who were with him in Corinth when he wrote the letter. What is the significance of this? It shows that Paul was a friend maker as well as a soul winner. He did not try to live an isolated life; he had friends in the Lord, and he appreciated them. They were a help to him personally and to his ministry. In my own reading of Christian biography, I have discovered that the servants whom God has used the most were people who could make friends. They multiplied themselves in the lives of their friends and associates in the ministry. While there may be a place for the secluded saint who lives alone with God, it is my conviction that most of us need each other. We are sheep, and sheep flock together.

Some friends to greet (vv. 1–16). He began with Phebe, a member of the church at Cenchrea and the woman who carried the letter to the saints at Rome. Never did a messenger carry a more important letter. Cenchrea was the seaport of Corinth, so Phebe was probably won to Christ during Paul's year and a half of ministry in Corinth. The word translated *servant* is the feminine of *deacon,* and some students believe she was a "deaconess" in the church. This is possible, because there were women in the early church who served by visiting the sick, assisting the young women, and helping the poor. Paul confessed that Phebe had been a helper (literally "protectress") of himself and other Christians. And he encouraged the church to care for her.

How we wish we had the details of the stories behind each of these names. We have met Priscilla and Aquila in the book of Acts (18:1–3, 18–19, 26). Where and when they risked their lives for Paul, we do not know, but we are glad they did it (see also 1 Cor. 16:19; 2 Tim 4:19). At the time of Paul's writing, they were in Rome and a church met in their house. In this chapter, Paul greeted a number of such assemblies (Rom. 16:10–11, 14–15).

Four persons are called "beloved" by Paul: Epaenetus (Rom. 16:5), Amplias (Rom. 16:8), Stachys (Rom. 16:9), and Persis (Rom. 16:12). Paul would remember Epaenetus in particular, for he was the first of the converts in Asia. Apparently he belonged to the household of Stephanas, for in 1 Corinthians 16:15 these people are also called "the firstfruits of Achaia."

Andronicus and Junias are called "kinsmen," which may mean blood relatives of Paul, or only that they too were Jewish, possibly of the tribe of Benjamin like Paul. At one time they had been in prison with Paul. The word *apostle* here does not imply that they held the same office as Paul, but rather that they were "messengers" of the Lord. The word *apostle* has both a narrow and a broad meaning.

The Rufus mentioned in Romans 16:13 may be the same as the one named in Mark 15:21, but we cannot be certain. If so, then Simon's experience at Calvary led to his conversion and that of his household. Paul and Rufus were not related. "His mother and mine" means only that Rufus's mother had been like a mother to Paul (see Mark 10:30).

This list shows the parts that people played in Paul's ministry and the ministry of the churches. Phebe was a "succourer" of many. Priscilla and Aquila were "helpers" and "laid down their own necks" for Paul. The conversion of Epaenetus led to the salvation of others in Asia. Mary "bestowed much labour." Andronicus and Junias went to prison with Paul. One can only give thanks for these devoted saints who fulfilled their ministries to the glory of God. May we follow in their train!

Some foes to avoid (vv. 17–20). Not everyone was working with Paul for the spreading of the gospel. There were some who, for selfish reasons, were dividing the churches by teaching false doctrine. These people were probably the same Judaizers who had given Paul trouble in other churches (see Phil. 3:17–21). Instead of preaching the truth, these men spread their own religious propaganda, using deceit and clever speeches. We have the same problem today, and Christians must beware of false teachers. They come to your front door with magazines, books, and tapes, trying to convince you that they are teaching the truth. Paul gives two instructions: Mark them (identify them), and avoid them.

It is a matter of obedience to the Lord and testimony to others. The issue is not making or keeping friends, but pleasing the Lord and maintaining a consistent testimony. Romans 16:20 suggests that these false teachers really come from Satan, and one day even he shall be completely defeated.

Some faithful servants to honor (vv. 21–27). What a roll call of heroes! Timothy was mentioned often in the book of Acts and the Epistles. He was Paul's "son in the faith" and labored with Paul in many difficult places (see Phil. 2:19–24). Lucius was a fellow Jew, as were Jason and Sosipater. We have no proof that this is the same Jason who protected Paul in Thessalonica (Acts 17:1–9). That Jason was probably a Gentile.

Tertius was the secretary who wrote the letter as Paul dictated it. Gaius was the man in whose home Paul was residing at Corinth. First Corinthians 1:14 told how Paul won Gaius to Christ and baptized him when he founded the church in Corinth. Apparently there was an assembly of believers meeting in his house. Erastus held a high office in the city, probably the treasurer. The gospel reached into high places in Corinth as well as into low places (1 Cor. 1:26–31; 6:9–11).

Romans 16:24 was probably written by Paul's own hand, since this was his "official seal" in every letter (see 2 Thess. 3:17–18).

The closing benediction is the longest one Paul ever wrote. It reflects his special ministry to the Gentiles. "The mystery" has to do with God's program of uniting believing Jews and Gentiles in the one body, the church (see Eph. 3). This was Paul's special message. It was because of this message that the Judaizers persecuted Paul, because they wanted to maintain Jewish privileges. Both Jews and Gentiles in the Roman churches needed to know what God's program was. Some of this Paul had explained in Romans 9—11.

Christians are established by the truth, which explains why Paul wrote this letter: to explain God's plan of salvation to Christians so they would be established, and so they would share the truth with the lost. After all, we cannot really share with others something we do not have ourselves.

This means that our own study of Romans should make us more stable in the faith, and more excited to share Christ with others. And the result? "To God only wise, be glory through Jesus Christ for ever."

QUESTIONS FOR PERSONAL REFLECTION
OR GROUP DISCUSSION

1. As you read Romans 15—16, what specific ministries did you see mentioned? Which of these resonate with you?

2. Since Jesus Christ is our supreme example of ministry, what characteristics of His ministry should we try to imitate?

3. What are five characteristics of Paul's ministry?

4. What is the significance of so many personal greetings?

5. Why did Paul give such a long benediction (16:17–27)?

6. How can we be more involved in a ministry to believers in the contemporary church?

7. What was the purpose of signs and wonders in Paul's ministry? Could this occur today? What other types of miracles have you heard of or seen?

8. If you were out of town and writing a letter to your church, who would you greet and what would you say to them?

9. What have you learned through the book of Romans that has been particularly helpful to you?

10. How will you begin, or continue, to practice these truths in your life? Pray daily and ask God for help in this.

The "BE" series . . .

For years pastors and lay leaders have embraced Warren W. Wiersbe's very accessible commentary of the Bible through the individual "BE" series. Through the work of David C. Cook Global Mission, the "BE" series is part of a library of books made available to indigenous Christian workers. These are men and women who are called by God to grow the kingdom through their work with the local church worldwide. Here are a few of their remarks as to how Dr. Wiersbe's writings have benefited their ministry.

"Most Christian books I see are priced too high for me . . .
I received a collection that included 12 Wiersbe
commentaries a few months ago and I have
read every one of them.
I use them for my personal devotions every day and they
are incredibly helpful for preparing sermons.
The contribution David C. Cook is making to the
church in India is amazing."
—Pastor E. M. Abraham, Hyderabad, India